KINDS OF MINDS

KINDS OF MINDS

....

Toward an Understanding of Consciousness

DANIEL C. DENNETT

📖 BasicBooks

A Division of HarperCollins*Publishers*

The Science Masters Series is a global publishing venture consisting of original science books written by leading scientists and published by a worldwide team of twenty-six publishers assembled by John Brockman. The series was conceived by Anthony Cheetham of Orion Publishers and John Brockman of Brockman Inc., a New York literary agency, and developed in coordination with BasicBooks.

•••••••

The Science Masters name and marks are owned by and licensed to the publisher by Brockman Inc.

•••••••

•••••••

Published by BasicBooks
A Division of HarperCollinsPublishers, Inc.

•••••••

•••••••

Designed by Joan Greenfield

•••••••

ISBN 0-465-07351-4 (pbk.)

•••••••

97 98 99 00 01 ❖/RRD 10 9 8 7 6 5 4 3 2 1

CONTENTS

v

I am a philosopher, not a scientist, and we philosophers are better at questions than answers. I haven't begun by insulting myself and my discipline, in spite of first appearances. Finding better questions to ask, and breaking old habits and traditions of asking, is a very difficult part of the grand human project of understanding ourselves and our world. Philosophers can make a fine contribution to this investigation, exploiting their professionally honed talents as question critics, provided they keep an open mind and restrain themselves from trying to answer all the questions from "obvious" first principles. There are many ways of asking questions about different kinds of minds, and my way—the way I will introduce in this book—changes almost daily, getting refined and enlarged, corrected and revised, as I learn of new discoveries, new theories, new problems. I will introduce the set of fundamental assumptions that hold my way together and give it a stable and recognizable pattern, but the most exciting parts of this way are at the changeable fringes of the pattern, where the action is. The main point of this book is to present the questions I'm asking *right now*—and some of them will probably lead nowhere, so let the reader beware. But my way of asking questions has a pretty good track record over the years, evolving quite smoothly to incorporate new discoveries, some of which were provoked by my earlier questions. Other philosophers have offered rival ways of asking the questions about minds, but the most influential of these ways, in spite of their initial attractiveness, lead to self-contradictions, quandaries, or blank walls of mystery, as I will demonstrate. So it is with confidence that I recommend my current candidates for the good questions.

Our minds are complex fabrics, woven from many different strands and incorporating many different designs. Some of these elements are as old as life itself, and others are as new as today's technology. Our minds are just like the minds of other animals in many respects and utterly unlike them in others. An evolutionary perspective can help us see how and why these elements of minds came to take on the shapes they have, but no single straight run through time, "from microbes to man," will reveal the moment of arrival of each new thread. So in what follows I have had to weave back and forth between simple and complex minds, reaching back again and again for themes that must be added, until eventually we arrive at something that is recognizably a human mind. Then we can look back, one more time, to survey the differences encountered and assess some of their implications.

Early drafts of this book were presented as the Agnes Cuming Lectures at University College, Dublin, and in my public lectures as Erskine Fellow at Canterbury University, Christchurch, New Zealand, in May and June of 1995. I want to thank the faculty and students at those institutions, whose constructive discussions helped make the final draft almost unrecognizably different, and (I trust) better. I also want to thank Marc Hauser, Alva Noë, Wei Cui, Shannon Densmore, Tom Schuman, Pascal Buckley, Jerry Lyons, Sara Lippincott, and my students in "Language and Mind" at Tufts, who read and vigorously criticized the penultimate draft.

Tufts University
December 20, 1995

··

CHAPTER 1

WHAT KINDS OF MINDS ARE THERE?

KNOWING YOUR OWN MIND
········

Can we ever really know what is going on in someone else's mind? Can a woman ever know what it is like to be a man? What experiences does a baby have during childbirth? What experiences, if any, does a fetus have in its mother's womb? And what of nonhuman minds? What do horses think about? Why aren't vultures nauseated by the rotting carcasses they eat? When a fish has a hook sticking through its lip, does it hurt the fish as much as it would hurt you, if you had a hook sticking through your lip? Can spiders think, or are they just tiny robots, mindlessly making their elegant webs? For that matter, why couldn't a robot—if it was fancy enough—be conscious? There are robots that can move around and manipulate things almost as adeptly as spiders; could a more complicated robot feel pain, and worry about its future, the way a person can? Or is there some unbridgeable chasm separating the robots (and maybe the spiders and insects and other "clever" but mindless creatures) from those animals that have minds? Could it be that all animals except human beings are really mindless robots? René Descartes notoriously maintained this in the seventeenth century. Might he have been dead wrong? Could it be that all animals, and even plants—and even bacteria—have minds?

Or, to swing to the other extreme, are we so sure that all human beings have minds? Maybe (to take the most extreme case of all) you're the only mind in the universe; maybe everything else, including the apparent author of this book, is a mere mindless machine. This strange idea first occurred to me when I was a young child, and perhaps it did to you as well. Roughly a third of my students claim that they, too, invented it on their own and mulled it over when they were children. They are often amused to learn that it's such a common philosophical hypothesis that it has a name—*solipsism* (from Latin for "myself alone"). Nobody ever takes solipsism seriously for long, as far as we know, but it does raise an important challenge: *if* we know that solipsism is silly—*if* we know that there are other minds—how do we know?

What kinds of minds are there? And how do we know? The first question is about what exists—about *ontology*, in philosophical parlance; the second question is about our knowledge—about *epistemology*. The goal of this book is not to answer these two questions once and for all, but rather to show why these questions have to be answered together. Philosophers often warn against confusing ontological questions with epistemological questions. What exists is one thing, they say, and what we can know about it is something else. There may be things that are completely unknowable to us, so we must be careful not to treat the limits of our knowledge as sure guides to the limits of what there is. I agree that this is good general advice, but I will argue that we already know enough about minds to know that one of the things that makes them different from everything else in the universe is the *way* we know about them. For instance, you know you have a mind and you know you have a brain, but these are different kinds of knowledge. You know you have a brain the way you know you have a spleen: by hearsay. You've never seen your spleen or your brain (I would bet), but since the textbooks tell you that all normal human beings have one of each, you conclude that you almost certainly have one of each as well. You are more intimately acquainted with your mind—so intimately that you might even say that you *are* your mind. (That's what Descartes said: he said he was a mind, a *res cogitans,* or thinking thing.) A book or a teacher might tell you what a mind is, but you wouldn't have to take anybody's word for the claim that you had one. If it occurred to you to wonder whether you were normal and had a mind as other people do, you would immediately realize, as Descartes pointed out, that your very wondering this wonder demonstrated beyond all doubt that you did indeed have a mind.

This suggests that each of us knows exactly one mind from the inside, and no two of us know the same mind from the inside. No other kind of thing is known about in that way. And yet this whole discussion so far has been conducted in terms of how *we* know—you and I. It presupposes that solipsism is false. The more we—we—reflect on this presupposition, the more unavoidable it appears. There couldn't be just one mind—or at least not just one mind like *our* minds.

WE MIND-HAVERS, WE MINDERS
········

If we want to consider the question of whether nonhuman animals have minds, we have to start by asking whether they have minds in some regards like ours, since these are the only minds we know anything about—at this point. (Try asking yourself whether nonhuman animals have flurbs. You can't even know what the question is, if you don't know what a flurb is supposed to be. Whatever else a mind is, it is supposed to be something like our minds; otherwise we wouldn't call it a mind.) So our minds, the only minds *we* know from the outset, are the standard with which we must begin. Without this agreement, we'll just be fooling ourselves, talking rubbish without knowing it.

When *I* address *you*, I include us both in the class of mind-havers. This unavoidable starting point creates, or acknowledges, an in-group, a class of privileged characters, set off against everything else in the universe. This is almost too obvious to notice, so deeply enshrined is it in our thinking and talking, but I must dwell on it. When there's a *we*, you are not alone; solipsism is false; there's company present. This comes out particularly clearly if we consider some curious variations:

"We left Houston at dawn, headin' down the road—just me and my truck."

Strange. If this fellow thinks his truck is such a worthy companion that it deserves shelter under the umbrella of "we," he must be very lonely. Either that, or his truck must have been customized in ways that would be the envy of roboticists everywhere. In contrast, "we—just me and my dog" doesn't startle us at all, but "we—just me and my oyster" is hard to take seriously. In other words, we're pretty sure that dogs have minds, and we're dubious that oysters do.

Membership in the class of things that have minds provides an all-important guarantee: the guarantee of a certain sort of moral standing. Only mind-havers can care; only mind-havers can mind what happens. If I do something to you that you don't want me to do, this has moral significance. It matters, because it matters to you. It may not matter much, or your interests may be overridden for all sorts of reasons, or (if I'm punishing you justly for a misdeed of yours) the fact that you care may actually count *in favor* of my deed. In any event, your caring automatically counts for something in the moral equation. If flowers have minds, then what we do to flowers can matter *to them*, and not just to those who care about what happens to flowers. If nobody cares, then it doesn't matter what happens to flowers.

There are some who would disagree; they would insist that the flowers had some moral standing even if nothing with a mind knew of or cared about their existence. Their beauty, for instance, no matter how unappreciated, is a good thing in itself, and hence should not be destroyed, other things being equal. This is not the view that the beauty of these flowers matters *to God*, for instance, or that it *might* matter to some being whose presence is undetectable by us. It is the view that the beauty matters, *even though it matters to no one*—not to the flowers themselves and not to God or anybody else. I remain unpersuaded, but rather than dismiss this view outright I will note that it is controversial and not widely shared. In contrast, it takes no special pleading at all to get most people to agree that something with a mind has interests that matter. That's why people are so concerned, morally, about the question of what has a mind: any proposed adjustment in the boundary of the class of mind-havers has major ethical significance.

We might make mistakes. We might endow mindless things with minds, or we might ignore a mindful thing in our midst. These mistakes would not be equal. To overattribute minds—to "make friends with" your houseplants or lie awake at night worrying about the welfare of the computer asleep on your desk—is, at worst, a silly error of credulity. To underattribute minds—to disregard or discount or deny the experience, the suffering and joy, the thwarted ambitions and frustrated desires of a mind-having person or animal—would be a terrible sin. After all, how would *you* feel if you were treated as an inanimate object? (Notice how this rhetorical question appeals to *our* shared status as mind-havers.)

In fact, both errors could have serious moral consequences. If we overattributed minds (if, for instance, we got it into our heads that since bacteria had minds, we couldn't justify killing them), this might lead us to sacrifice the interests of many legitimate interest-holders—our friends, our pets, ourselves—for nothing of genuine moral importance. The abortion debate hinges on just such a quandary; some think it's obvious that a ten-week-old fetus has a mind, and others think it's obvious that it does not. If it does not, then the path is open to argue that it has no more interests than, say, a gangrenous leg or an abscessed tooth—it can be destroyed to save the life (or just to suit the interests) of the mind-haver of which it is a part. If it does already have a mind, then, whatever we decide, we obviously have to consider *its* interests along with the interests of its temporary host. In between these extreme positions lies the real quandary: the fetus will soon develop a mind if left undisturbed, so when do we start counting its *prospective* interests? The relevance of mind-having to the question of moral standing is especially clear in these cases, since if the fetus in question is known to be anencephalic (lacking a brain), this dramatically changes the issue for most people. Not for all. (I am not attempting to settle these moral issues here, but just to show how a common moral opinion amplifies our interest in these questions way beyond normal curiosity.)

The dictates of morality and scientific method pull in opposite directions here. The ethical course is to err on the side of overattribution, just to be safe. The scientific course is to put the burden of proof on the attribution. As a scientist, you can't just *declare*, for instance, that the presence of glutamate molecules (a basic neurotransmitter involved in signaling between nerve cells) amounts to the presence of mind; you have to prove it, against a background in which the "null hypothesis" is that mind is not present. (*Innocent until proven guilty* is the null hypothesis in our criminal law.) There is substantial disagreement among scientists about which species have what sorts of mind, but even those scientists who are the most ardent champions of consciousness in animals accept this burden of proof—and think they can meet it, by devising and confirming theories that show which animals are conscious. But no such theories are yet confirmed, and in the meantime we can appreciate the discomfort of those who see this agnostic, wait-and-see policy as jeopardizing the moral status of creatures they are *sure* are conscious.

Suppose the question before us were not about the minds of pigeons or bats but about the minds of left-handed people or people with red hair. We would be deeply offended to be told that it had yet to be proved that this category of living thing had the wherewithal for entry into the privileged class of mind-havers. Many people are similarly outraged by the demand for proof of mind-having in nonhuman species, but if they're honest with themselves they will grant that they, too, see the need for such proof in the case of, say, jellyfish or amoebas or daisies; so we agree on the principle, and they're just taking umbrage at its application to creatures so very much like us. We can allay their misgivings somewhat by agreeing that we should err well on the side of inclusiveness in all our policies, until the facts are in; still, the price you must pay for scientific confirmation of your favorite hypothesis about animal minds is the risk of scientific disconfirmation.

WORDS AND MINDS
········

It is beyond serious dispute, however, that you and I each have a mind. How do I know you have a mind? Because anybody who can understand my words is automatically addressed by my pronoun "you," and only things with minds can understand. There are computer-driven devices that can read books for the blind: they convert a page of visible text into a stream of audible words, but they don't understand the words they read and hence are not addressed by any "you" they encounter; it passes right through them and addresses whoever listens to—and understands—the stream of spoken words. That's how I know that you, gentle reader/listener, have a mind. So do I. Take my word for it.

In fact that's what we routinely do: we take each other's words as settling beyond any reasonable doubt the question of whether we each have minds. Why should words be so convincing? Because they are such powerful resolvers of doubts and ambiguities. You see somebody coming toward you, scowling and waving an ax. You wonder, What's his problem? Is he going to attack me? Is he mistaking me for somebody else? Ask him. Perhaps he will confirm your worst fears, or perhaps he will tell you he has given up trying to unlock his car (which you're standing in front of) and has returned with his ax to break the window. You may not believe him when he says it's his car, not somebody else's, but further conversation—if you decide not to run away—is bound to resolve your doubts and clarify the situation in ways that would be all but impossible if you and he were unable to communicate verbally. Suppose you try asking him, but it turns out that he doesn't speak your language. Perhaps you will then both resort to gestures and miming. These techniques, used with ingenuity, will take you far, but they're a poor substitute for language—just reflect on how eagerly you would both seek to confirm your hard-won understanding if a bilingual interpreter were to come along. A few relayed questions and answers would not just allay any residual uncertainty but would add details that could not be conveyed in any other way: "When he saw you put one hand on your chest and push out with your other hand, he thought you meant that you were ill; he was trying to ask if you wanted him to take you to a doctor once he'd broken the window and retrieved his keys. That business with his fingers in his ears was his attempt to convey a stethoscope." Ah, it all falls into place now, thanks to a few words.

People often emphasize the difficulty of accurate and reliable translation between human languages. Human cultures, we are told, are too different, too "incommensurable," to permit the meanings available to one speaker to be perfectly shared with another. No doubt translation always falls somewhat short of perfection, but this may not matter much in the larger scheme of things. Perfect translation may be impossible, but good translation is achieved every day—routinely, in fact. Good translation can be objectively distinguished from not-so-good translation and from bad translation, and it permits all human beings, regardless of race, culture, age, gender, or experience, to unite more closely with one another than individuals of any other species can. We human beings share a subjective world—and know that we do—in a way that is entirely beyond the capacities of any other creatures on the planet, because we can talk to one another. Human beings who don't (yet) have a language in which to communicate are the exception, and that's why we have a particular problem figuring out what it's like to be a newborn baby or a deaf-mute.

Conversation unites us. We can all know a great deal about what it's like to be a Norwegian fisherman or a Nigerian taxi driver, an eighty-year-old nun or a five-year-old boy blind from birth, a chess master or a prostitute or a fighter pilot. We can know much more about these topics than we can know about what it's like (if anything) to be a dolphin, a bat, or even a chimpanzee. No matter how different from one another we people are, scattered around the globe, we can explore our differences and communicate about them. No matter how similar to one another wildebeests are, standing shoulder to shoulder in a herd, they cannot know much of anything about their similarities, let alone their differences. They cannot compare notes. They can have similar experiences, side by side, but they really cannot share experiences the way we do.

Some of you may doubt this. Can't animals "instinctively" understand each other in ways we human beings cannot fathom? Certainly some authors have said so. Consider, for instance, Elizabeth Marshall Thomas, who imagines, in *The Hidden Life of Dogs* (1993), that dogs enjoy a wise understanding of their own ways. One example: "For reasons known to dogs but not to us, many dog mothers won't mate with their sons." (p. 76). Their instinctive resistance to such inbreeding is not in doubt, but what gives her the idea that dogs have any more insight into the reasons for their instincts than we have into ours? There are many things we feel strongly and instinctively disinclined to do, with no inkling about why we feel that way. To suppose without proof that dogs have more insight into their urges than we do is to ignore the null hypothesis in an unacceptable way—if we are asking a scientific question. As we shall see, very simple organisms may be attuned to their environments and to each other in strikingly apt ways without having the slightest appreciation of their attunement. We *already* know from conversation, however, that people are typically capable of a very high order of understanding of themselves and others.

Of course, we can be fooled. People often emphasize the

difficulty of determining whether a speaker is sincere. Words, by being the most powerful tools of communication, are also the most powerful tools of deception and manipulation. But while it may be easy to lie, it's almost as easy to catch a liar—especially when the lies get large and the logistical problem of maintaining the structure of falsehood overwhelms the liar. In fantasy, we can conjure up infinitely powerful deceivers, but the deceptions that are "possible in principle" to such an evil demon can be safely ignored in the real world. It would be just too difficult to make up that much falsehood and maintain it consistently. We *know* that people the world over have much the same likes and dislikes, hopes and fears. We know that they enjoy recollecting favorite events in their lives. We know that they all have rich episodes of waking fantasy, in which they rearrange and revise the details deliberately. We know that they have obsessions, nightmares, and hallucinations. We know that they can be reminded by an aroma or a melody of a specific event in their lives, and that they often talk to themselves silently, without moving their lips. Long before there was scientific psychology, long before there was meticulous observation of and experimentation on human subjects, this was all common knowledge. We have known these facts about people since ancient times, because we have talked it over with them, at great length. We know nothing comparable about the mental lives of any other species, because we can't talk it over with them. We may think we know, but it takes scientific investigation to confirm or refute our traditional hunches.

THE PROBLEM OF INCOMMUNICATIVE MINDS
········

It's very hard to tell what somebody is thinking who won't discuss it—or who can't, for one reason or another. But we normally suppose that such incommunicative folks are indeed thinking—that they do have minds—even if we can't confirm the details. This much is obvious, if only because we can readily imagine ourselves in a situation in which we would steadfastly refuse to communicate, all the while thinking our private thoughts, perhaps reflecting with amusement on the difficulties that observers were having in figuring out what, if anything, was going on in our minds. Talking, no matter how conclusive its presence may be, is not necessary for having a mind. From this obvious fact we are tempted to draw a problematic conclusion: there could be entities who do have minds but who cannot tell us what they're thinking—not because they're paralyzed or suffering from aphasia (the inability to communicate verbally due to localized brain damage), but because they have no capacity for language at all. Why do I say this is a problematic conclusion?

First let's consider the case to be made in its favor. Surely, tradition and common sense declare, there are minds without language. Surely our ability to discuss with others what is going on in our minds is just a peripheral talent, in the sense in which one speaks of a computer's laser printer as a peripheral device (the computer can go right on computing without a printer attached). Surely nonhuman animals—at least, some of them—have mental lives. Surely human infants before they acquire language, and human deaf-mutes—even those rare deaf-mutes who have never acquired even sign language—have minds. Surely. These minds may doubtless differ in many hard-to-fathom ways from *our* minds—the minds of those who can understand a conversation such as this—but surely they *are* minds. Our royal road to the knowledge of other minds—language—does not extend to them, but this is just a limitation on our knowledge, not a limitation on their minds. The prospect arises, then, that there are minds whose contents are systematically inaccessible to our curiosity—unknowable, uncheckable, impenetrable by any investigation.

The traditional response to this prospect is to embrace it. Yes indeed, minds are the ultimate *terra incognita*, beyond the reach of all science and—in the case of languageless minds—beyond all empathetic conversation as well. So what? A little humility ought to temper our curiosity. Don't confuse ontological questions (about what exists) with epistemological questions (about how we know about it). We must grow comfortable with this wonderful fact about what is off-limits to inquiry.

But before we get comfortable with this conclusion, we need to consider the implications of some other facts about our own case that are just as obvious. We find that we often do clever things without thinking at all; we do them "automatically," or "unconsciously." What is it like, for instance, to use information about the optic flow of shapes in peripheral vision to adjust the length of your stride as you walk across rough terrain? The answer is, It isn't like anything. You can't pay attention to this process even if you try. What is it like to notice, while sound asleep, that your left arm has become twisted into a position in which it is putting undue strain on your left shoulder? Like nothing; it is not part of your experience. You swiftly and unconsciously shift to a more "comfortable" position, without any interruption of your sleep. If we are asked to discuss these putative parts of our mental lives, we draw a blank; whatever happened in us to govern these clever behaviors wasn't a part of our mental lives at all. So another prospect to consider is that among the creatures who lack language, there are some that do not have minds at all, but do everything "automatically" or "unconsciously."

The traditional response to this prospect, too, is to embrace it. Yes indeed, some creatures entirely lack minds. Surely bacteria are mindless, and so, probably, are amoebas and starfish. Quite possibly even ants, for all their clever activity, are mere mindless automata, trundling about in the world without the slightest experience or thought. What about trout? What about chickens? What about rats? We may never be able to tell where to draw the line between those creatures that have minds and those that do not, but this is just another aspect of the unavoidable limitations on our knowledge. Such facts may be systematically unknowable, not just hard to uncover.

Here, then, are two sorts of supposedly unknowable facts: facts about what is going on in those who have minds but no way of talking about their thoughts, and facts about which creatures have minds at all. These two varieties of off-limits ignorance are not equally easy to accept. The differences *between minds* might be differences whose major outlines were readily discernible to objective observers but whose minor details became harder and harder to determine—a case of diminishing returns for labor invested. The unknown leftovers would not be mysteries but just inevitable gaps in a richly informative but finite catalog of similarities and differences. The differences between minds would then be like the differences between languages, or styles of music or art— inexhaustible in the limit, but approachable to any degree of approximation you like. But the difference between having a mind and not having a mind at all—between being something with its own subjective point of view and being something that is all outside and no inside, like a rock or a discarded sliver of fingernail—is apparently an all-or-nothing difference. It is much harder to accept the idea that no amount of further investigation will ever tell us *whether there is anyone there to care* inside a lobster's shell, for instance, or behind the shiny façade of a robot.

The suggestion that such a morally important sort of fact could be systematically unknowable by us is simply intolerable. It means that no matter what investigations we conducted, we might, for all we could know, be sacrificing the genuine moral interests of some for the entirely illusory benefit of mindless others. Unavoidable ignorance of the consequences is often a legitimate excuse when we find we have unwittingly produced some harm in the world, but if we must declare ourselves at the outset to be unavoidably ignorant of the very basis of all moral thinking, morality becomes a sham. Fortunately, this conclusion is as incredible as it is intolerable. The claim that, say, left-handed people are unconscious zombies that may be dismantled as if they were bicycles is preposterous. So, at the other extreme, is the claim that bacteria suffer, or that carrots mind being plucked unceremoniously from their earthy homes. Obviously, we can know to a moral certainty (which is all that matters) that some things have minds and other things don't.

But we don't yet know *how* we know these facts; the strength of our intuitions about such cases is no guarantee of their reliability. Consider a few cases, beginning with this remark by the evolutionist Elaine Morgan:

> The heart-stopping thing about the new-born is that, from minute one, there is somebody there. Anyone who bends over the cot and gazes at it is being gazed back at. (1995, p. 99)

As an observation about how we human observers instinctively react to eye contact, this is right on target, but it thereby shows how easily we can be misled. We can be fooled by a robot, for instance. At the Artificial Intelligence

Lab at MIT, Rodney Brooks and Lynn Andrea Stein have assembled a team of roboticists and others (myself included) to build a humanoid robot, named Cog. Cog is made of metal and silicon and glass, like other robots, but the design is so different, so much more like the design of a human being, that Cog may someday become the world's first conscious robot. Is a conscious robot possible? I have defended a theory of consciousness, the Multiple Drafts Model (1991), that implies that a conscious robot is possible in principle, and Cog is being designed with that distant goal in mind. But Cog is nowhere near being conscious yet. Cog cannot yet see or hear or feel at all, but its bodily parts can already move in unnervingly humanoid ways. Its eyes are tiny video cameras, which *saccade*—dart—to focus on any person who enters the room and then track that person as he or she moves. Being tracked in this way is an oddly unsettling experience, even for those in the know. Staring into Cog's eyes while Cog stares mindlessly back can be quite "heart-stopping" to the uninitiated, but there is nobody there—not yet, in any case. Cog's arms, unlike those of standard robots both real and cinematic, move swiftly and flexibly, like your arms; when you press on Cog's extended arm, it responds with an uncannily humanoid resistance that makes you want to exclaim, in stock horror-movie fashion, "It's alive! It's alive!" It isn't, but the intuition to the contrary is potent.

While we're imagining arms, let's consider a variation with a different moral: A man's arm has been cut off in a terrible accident, but the surgeons think they can reattach it. While it is lying there, still soft and warm, on the operating table, does it feel pain? (If so, we should inject some novocaine into it—especially if we plan to use a scalpel to cut back any tissue on the amputated arm before attempting the reunion.) A silly suggestion, you reply; it takes a mind to feel pain, and as long as the arm is not attached to a body with a mind, whatever you do to the arm can't cause suffering in any mind. But perhaps the arm has a mind of its own. Perhaps it has always had one but has just been unable to talk to us about it! Well, why not? It does have a substantial number of nerve cells in it, still firing away. If we found a whole organism with that many active nerve cells in it, we would be strongly inclined to suppose that it was capable of experiencing pain, even if it couldn't express itself in terms we could understand. Here intuitions collide: arms don't have minds, in spite of containing plenty of the processes and materials that tend to persuade us that some nonhuman animals do have minds.

Is it behavior that counts? Suppose you pinched the thumb of the amputated arm and it pinched you back! Would you then decide to give it novocaine? If not, why not? Because its reaction would have to be an "automatic" reflex? How can you be so sure? Is it something about the organization of those nerve cells that makes the difference?

These puzzle cases are fun to think about, and we learn important facts about our naive concepts of mind when we try to figure out why our intuitions line up the way they do, but there must be a better way of investigating kinds of minds—and nonminds that might fool us. The defeatist conviction that we will never know should be postponed indefinitely, saved as a last-gasp conclusion to be reached only after we have actually exhausted all other avenues and not just imagined doing so. There may be surprises and illuminations awaiting us.

One prospect to consider, whether or not in the end we rule it out, is that perhaps language is not so peripheral to minds after all. Perhaps the kind of mind you get when you add language to it is so different from the kind of mind you can have without language that calling them both minds is a mistake. Perhaps, in other words, our sense that there are riches in the minds of other creatures—riches inaccessible to *us* but not, of course, to *them*—is an illusion. The philosopher

Ludwig Wittgenstein famously said, "If a lion could talk, we could not understand him." (1958, p. 223) That's one possibility, no doubt, but it diverts our attention from another possibility: if a lion could talk, we could understand him just fine—with the usual sorts of effort required for translation between different languages—but our conversations with him would tell us next to nothing about the minds of ordinary lions, since his language-equipped mind would be so different. It *might* be that adding language to a lion's "mind" would be *giving* him a mind for the first time! Or it might not. In either case, we should investigate the prospect and not just assume, with tradition, that the minds of nonspeaking animals are really rather like ours.

If we are to find some alternative path of investigation, instead of just relying uncritically on our pretheoretical intuitions, how might we begin? Let's consider the historical, evolutionary path. There haven't always been minds. *We* have minds, but we haven't existed forever. We evolved from beings with simpler minds (if minds they were), who evolved from beings with still simpler candidates for minds. And there was a time, four or five billion years ago, when there weren't any minds at all, simple or complex—at least, not on this planet. Which innovations occurred in what order, and why? The major steps are clear, even if the details about dates and places can be only speculative. Once we've told that story, we will at least have a framework in which to try to place our quandaries. Perhaps we will want to distinguish classes of pseudominds, or protominds, or semiminds, or hemi-semi-demi-minds from the real thing. Whatever we decide to call these ancestral arrangements, perhaps we can agree upon a scale on which they mount, and the conditions and principles that created the scale in the first place. The next chapter develops some tools for this investigation.

··

CHAPTER 2

INTENTIONALITY:
THE INTENTIONAL SYSTEMS APPROACH

> I notice something and seek a reason for it: this
> means originally: I seek an intention in it, and
> above all someone who has intentions, a sub-
> ject, a doer: every event a deed—formerly one
> saw intentions in all events, this is our oldest
> habit. Do animals also possess it?
>
> Friedrich Nietzsche, *The Will to Power*

SIMPLE BEGINNINGS:
THE BIRTH OF AGENCY*

········

No grain of sand has a mind; a grain of sand is too simple.
Even simpler, no carbon atom or water molecule has a mind.
I expect no serious disagreement about that. But what about
larger molecules? A virus is a single huge molecule, a macromolecule composed of hundreds of thousands or even millions of parts, depending on how small the parts are that we

········

*Portions of this section are drawn from my 1995 book, *Darwin's
Dangerous Idea*, with revisions.

count. These atomic-level parts interact, in their obviously mindless ways, to produce some quite striking effects. Chief among these effects, from the point of view of our investigation, is *self-replication*. Some macromolecules have the amazing ability, if left floating in a suitably well-furnished medium, to mindlessly construct and then shed exact—or nearly exact—copies of themselves. DNA and its ancestor, RNA, are such macromolecules; they are the foundation of all life on this planet and hence a historical precondition for all minds—at least, all minds on this planet. For about a billion years before simple single-celled organisms appeared on earth, there were self-replicating macromolecules, ceaselessly mutating, growing, even repairing themselves, and getting better and better at it—and replicating over and over again.

This is a stupendous feat, still well beyond the capacity of any existing robot. Does that mean that such macromolecules have minds like ours? Certainly not. They're not even alive—they're just huge crystals, from the point of view of chemistry. These gigantic molecules are tiny machines—*macro*molecular *nano*technology. They are, in effect, natural robots. The possibility in principle of a self-replicating robot was mathematically demonstrated by John von Neumann, one of the inventors of the computer, whose brilliant design for a nonliving self-replicator anticipated many of the details of design and construction of RNA and DNA.

Through the microscope of molecular biology, we get to witness the birth of *agency*, in the first macromolecules that have enough complexity to *perform actions*, instead of just lying there *having effects*. Their agency is not fully fledged agency like ours. They know not what they do. We, in contrast, often know full well what we do. At our best—and at our worst—we human agents can perform *intentional* actions, after having deliberated consciously about the reasons for and against. Macromolecular agency is different;

there are reasons for what macromolecules do, but the macromolecules are unaware of those reasons. Their sort of agency is nevertheless the only possible ground from which the seeds of our kind of agency could grow.

There is something alien and vaguely repellent about the quasi agency we discover at this level—all that purposive hustle and bustle, and yet "there's nobody home." The molecular machines perform their amazing stunts, obviously exquisitely designed and just as obviously none the wiser about what they are doing. Consider this account of the activity of an RNA phage—a replicating virus and a modern-day descendant of the earliest self-replicating macromolecules:

First of all, the virus needs a material in which to pack and protect its own genetic information. Secondly, it needs a means of introducing its information into the host cell. Thirdly, it requires a mechanism for the specific replication of its information in the presence of a vast excess of host cell RNA. Finally, it must arrange for the proliferation of its information, a process that usually leads to the destruction of the host cell. . . . The virus even gets the cell to carry out its replication; its only contribution is one protein factor, specially adapted for the viral RNA. This enzyme does not become active until a "password" on the viral RNA is shown. When it sees this, it reproduces the viral RNA with great efficiency, while ignoring the very much greater number of RNA molecules of the host cell. Consequently the cell is soon flooded with viral RNA. This is packed into the virus' coat protein, which is also synthesized in large quantities, and finally the cell bursts and releases a multitude of progeny virus particles. All this is a programme that runs automatically and is rehearsed down to the smallest detail. (Eigen, 1992, p. 40)

The author, the molecular biologist Manfred Eigen, has helped himself to a rich vocabulary of agency words: in order to reproduce, the virus must "arrange for" the proliferation of its information, and in furthering this goal it creates an enzyme that "sees" its password and "ignores" other molecules. This is poetic license, to be sure; these words have had their meanings stretched for the occasion. But what an irresistible stretch! The agency words draw attention to the most striking features of the phenomena: these macromolecules are *systematic*. Their control systems are not just efficient at what they do; they are appropriately sensitive to variation, opportunistic, ingenious, devious. They can be "fooled," but only by novelties not regularly encountered by their ancestors.

These impersonal, unreflective, robotic, mindless little scraps of molecular machinery are the ultimate basis of all the agency, and hence meaning, and hence consciousness, in the world. It is rare for such a solid and uncontroversial scientific fact to have such potent implications for structuring all subsequent debate about something as controversial and mysterious as minds, so let's pause to remind ourselves of these implications.

There is no longer any serious informed doubt about this: *we are the direct descendants of these self-replicating robots*. We are mammals, and all mammals have descended from reptilian ancestors whose ancestors were fish whose ancestors were marine creatures rather like worms, who descended in turn from simpler multicelled creatures several hundred million years ago, who descended from single-celled creatures who descended from self-replicating macromolecules, about three billion years ago. There is just one family tree, on which all living things that have ever lived on this planet can be found—not just animals, but plants and algae and bacteria as well. You share a common ancestor with every chimpanzee, every worm, every blade of grass, every redwood tree. Among our progenitors, then, were macromolecules.

To put it vividly, your great-great-... grandmother *was* a robot! Not only are you descended from such macromolecular robots but you are composed of them: your hemoglobin molecules, your antibodies, your neurons, your vestibular-ocular reflex machinery—at every level of analysis from the molecular on up, your body (including your brain, of course) is found to be composed of machinery that dumbly does a wonderful, elegantly designed job.

We have ceased to shudder, perhaps, at the scientific vision of viruses and bacteria busily and mindlessly executing their subversive projects—horrid little automata doing their evil deeds. But we should not think that we can take comfort in the thought that *they* are alien invaders, so unlike the more congenial tissues that make up *us*. We are made of the same sorts of automata that invade us—no special halos of humanity distinguish your antibodies from the antigens they combat; your antibodies simply belong to the club that is you, so they fight on your behalf. The billions of neurons that band together to make your brain are cells, the same sort of biological entity as the germs that cause infections, or the yeast cells that multiply in the vat when beer is fermenting or in the dough when bread rises.

Each cell—a tiny agent that can perform a limited number of tasks—is about as mindless as a virus. Can it be that if enough of these dumb homunculi—little men—are put together the result will be a real, conscious person, with a genuine mind? According to modern science, there is no other way of making a real person. Now, it certainly does not follow from the fact that we are descended from robots that we are robots ourselves. After all, we are also direct descendants of fish, and we are not fish; we are direct descendants of bacteria, and we are not bacteria. But unless there is some secret extra ingredient in us (which is what dualists and vitalists used to think), we are *made of* robots—or, what comes to the same thing, we are each a collection of trillions of macromolecular machines. And all of these are ultimately descended from the original self-replicating macromolecules. So something made of robots *can* exhibit genuine consciousness, because you do if anything does.

To some people, all this seems shocking and unlikely, I realize, but I suspect that they haven't noticed how desperate the alternatives are. Dualism (the view that minds are composed of some nonphysical and utterly mysterious stuff) and vitalism (the view that living things contain some special physical but equally mysterious stuff—*élan vital*) have been relegated to the trash heap of history, along with alchemy and astrology. Unless you are also prepared to declare that the world is flat and the sun is a fiery chariot pulled by winged horses—unless, in other words, your defiance of modern science is quite complete—you won't find any place to stand and fight for these obsolete ideas. So let's see what story can be told with the conservative resources of science. Maybe the idea that our minds evolved from simpler minds is not so bad after all.

Our macromolecule ancestors (and that's exactly and unmetaphorically what they were: our ancestors) were agent*like* in some ways, as the quotation from Eigen makes clear, and yet in other ways they were undeniably passive, floating randomly around, pushed hither and yon—waiting for action with their guns cocked, you might say, but not waiting *hopefully* or *resolutely* or *intently*. Their jaws might have gaped, but they were as mindless as a steel trap.

What changed? Nothing sudden. Before our ancestors got minds, they got bodies. First, they became simple cells, or prokaryotes, and eventually the prokaryotes took in some invaders, or boarders, and thereby became complex cells— the eukaryotes. By this time, roughly a billion years after the first appearance of simple cells, our ancestors were already extraordinarily complex machines (made of machines made of machines), but they still didn't have minds. They were as passive and undirected in their trajectories as ever, but now they were equipped with many specialized subsystems, for extracting energy and material from the environment and protecting and repairing themselves when necessary.

The elaborate organization of all these coordinated parts was not very much like a mind. Aristotle had a name for it— or for its descendants: he called it a *nutritive soul*. A nutritive soul is not a thing; it is not, for instance, one of the microscopic subsystems floating around in the cytoplasm of a cell. It is a *principle of organization*; it is form, not substance, as Aristotle said. All living things—not only plants and animals but also unicellular organisms—have bodies that require a self-regulative and self-protective organization that can be differentially activated by different conditions. These organizations are brilliantly designed, by natural selection, and they are composed, at bottom, of lots of tiny passive switches that can be turned ON or OFF by equally passive conditions that the organisms encounter in their wanderings.

You yourself, like all other animals, have a nutritive soul—a self-regulative, self-protective organization—quite distinct from, and more ancient than, your nervous system: it consists of your metabolic system, your immune system, and the other staggeringly complex systems of self-repair and health maintenance in your body. The lines of communication used by these early systems were not nerves but blood vessels. Long before there were telephones and radios, there was the postal service, reliably if rather slowly transporting physical packages of valuable information around the world. And long before there were nervous systems in organisms, bodies relied on a low-tech postal system of sorts—the circulation of fluids within the body, reliably if rather slowly transporting valuable packages of information to where they were needed for control and self-maintenance. We see the descendants of this primordial postal system in both animals and plants. In animals, the bloodstream carries goods and waste, but it has also been, since the early days, an information highway. The motion of fluids within plants also provides a relatively rudimentary medium for getting signals from one part of the plant to another. But in animals, we can see a major design innovation: the evolution of simple nervous systems—ancestors of the autonomic nervous system—capable of swifter and more efficient information transmission but still devoted, in the main, to internal affairs. An autonomic nervous system is not a mind at all but rather a control system, more along the lines of the nutritive soul of a plant, that preserves the basic integrity of the living system.

We sharply distinguish these ancient systems from our minds, and yet, curiously, the closer we look at the details of their operation the more mindlike we find them to be! The little switches are like primitive sense organs, and the effects that are produced when these switches are turned ON and OFF are like intentional actions. How so? In being effects produced by *information*-modulated, *goal*-seeking systems. It is *as if* these cells and cell assemblies were tiny, simple-minded *agents*, specialized servants rationally furthering their particular obsessive causes by acting in the ways their perception of circumstances dictated. The world is teeming with such entities, ranging from the molecular to the continental in size and including not only "natural" objects, such as plants, animals, and their parts (and the parts of their parts), but also many human artifacts. Thermostats, for instance, are a familiar example of such simple pseudo-agents.

I call all these entities, from the simplest to the most complex, *intentional systems*, and I call the perspective from which their agenthood (pseudo or genuine) is made visible, the *intentional stance*.

ADOPTING THE INTENTIONAL STANCE
....

The intentional stance is the strategy of interpreting the behavior of an entity (person, animal, artifact, whatever) by treating it *as if* it were a rational agent who governed its "choice" of "action" by a "consideration" of its "beliefs" and "desires." These terms in scare-quotes have been stretched out of their home use in what's often called "folk psychology," the everyday psychological discourse we use to discuss the mental lives of our fellow human beings. The intentional stance is the attitude or perspective we routinely adopt toward one another, so adopting the intentional stance toward something else seems to be deliberately *anthropomorphizing* it. How could this possibly be a good idea?

I will try to show that if done with care, adopting the intentional stance is not just a good idea but the key to unraveling the mysteries of the mind—all kinds of minds. It is a method that exploits similarities in order to discover differences—the huge collection of differences that have accumulated between the minds of our ancestors and ours, and also between our minds and those of our fellow inhabitants of the planet. It must be used with caution; we must walk a tightrope between vacuous metaphor on the one hand and literal falsehood on the other. Improper use of the intentional stance can seriously mislead the unwary researcher, but properly understood, it can provide a sound and fruitful perspective in several different fields, exhibiting underlying unity in the phenomena and directing our attention to the crucial experiments that need to be conducted.

The basic strategy of the intentional stance is to treat the entity in question as an agent, in order to predict—and thereby explain, in one sense—its actions or moves. The distinctive features of the intentional stance can best be seen by contrasting it with two more basic stances or strategies of prediction: the *physical stance* and the *design stance*. The physical stance is simply the standard laborious method of the physical sciences, in which we use whatever we know about the laws of physics and the physical constitution of the things in question to devise our prediction. When I predict that a stone released from my hand will fall to the ground, I am using the physical stance. I don't attribute beliefs and desires to the stone; I attribute mass, or weight, to the stone, and rely on the law of gravity to yield my prediction. For things that are neither alive nor artifacts, the physical stance is the only available strategy, though it can be conducted at various levels of detail, from the subatomic to the astronomical. Explanations of why water bubbles when it boils, how mountain ranges come into existence, and where the energy in the sun comes from are explanations from the physical stance. Every physical thing, whether designed or alive or not, is subject to the laws of physics and hence behaves in ways that can be explained and predicted from the physical stance. If the thing I release from my hand is an alarm clock or a goldfish, I make the same prediction about its downward trajectory, on the same basis. And even a model airplane, or a bird, which may well take a different trajectory when released, behaves in ways that obey the laws of physics at every scale and at every moment.

Alarm clocks, being designed objects (unlike the rock), are also amenable to a fancier style of prediction—prediction from the design stance. The design stance is a wonderful shortcut, which we all use all the time. Suppose someone gives me a new digital alarm clock. It is a make and model quite novel to me, but a brief examination of its exterior buttons and displays convinces me that *if* I depress a few buttons just so, *then* some hours later the alarm clock will make a loud noise. I don't know what kind of noise it will be, but it will be sufficient to awaken me. I don't need to work out the specific physical laws that explain this marvelous regularity; I don't need to take the thing apart, weighing its parts and measuring the voltages. I simply *assume* that it has a particular design—the design we call an alarm clock—and that it will function properly, as designed. I'm prepared to risk quite a lot on this prediction—not my life, perhaps, but my waking up in time to get to my scheduled lecture or catch a train. Design-stance predictions are riskier than physical-stance predictions, because of the extra assumptions I have to take on board: that an entity *is* designed as I suppose it to be, and that it will operate according to that design—that is, it will not malfunction. Designed things are occasionally misdesigned, and sometimes they break. But this moderate price I pay in riskiness is more than compensated by the tremendous ease of prediction. Design-stance prediction, when applicable, is a low-cost, low-risk shortcut, enabling me to finesse the tedious application of my limited knowledge of physics. In fact we all routinely risk our lives on design-stance predictions: we unhesitatingly plug in and turn on electrical appliances that could kill us if miswired; we voluntarily step into buses we know will soon accelerate us to lethal speeds; we calmly press buttons in elevators we have never been in before.

Design-stance prediction works wonderfully on well-designed artifacts, but it also works wonderfully on Mother Nature's artifacts—living things and their parts. Long before the physics and chemistry of plant growth and reproduction were understood, our ancestors quite literally bet their lives on the reliability of their design-stance knowledge of what seeds were *supposed* to do when planted. *If* I press a few seeds into the ground just so, *then* in a few months, with a modicum of further care from me, there will be food here to eat.

We have just seen that design-stance predictions are risky, compared with physical-stance predictions (which are safe but tedious to work out), and an even riskier and swifter stance is the intentional stance. It can be viewed, if you like, as a subspecies of the design stance, in which the designed thing is an agent of sorts. Suppose we apply it to the alarm clock. This alarm clock is my servant; if I *command it* to wake me up, by *giving it to understand* a particular time of awakening, I can rely on its internal ability to *perceive* when that time has arrived and dutifully execute the action it has promised. As soon as it comes to *believe* that the time for noise is NOW, it will be "motivated," thanks to my earlier instructions, to act accordingly. No doubt the alarm clock is so simple that this fanciful anthropomorphism is, strictly speaking, unnecessary for our understanding of why it does what it does—but notice that this is how we might explain to a child how to use an alarm clock: "You tell it when you want it to wake you up, and it remembers to do so, by making a loud noise."

Adoption of the intentional stance is more useful—indeed, well-nigh obligatory—when the artifact in question is much more complicated than an alarm clock. My favorite example is a chess-playing computer. There are hundreds of different computer programs that can turn a computer, whether it's a laptop or a supercomputer, into a chess player. For all their differences at the physical level and the design level, these computers all succumb neatly to the same simple strategy of interpretation: just think of them as rational agents who *want* to win, and who *know* the rules and principles of chess and the positions of the pieces on the board. Instantly your problem of predicting and interpreting their behavior is made vastly easier than it would be if you tried to use the physical or the design stance. At any moment in the chess game, simply look at the chessboard and draw up a list of all the legal moves available to the computer when it is its turn to play (there will usually be several dozen candidates). Why restrict yourself to legal moves? Because, you reason, it wants to play winning chess and knows that it must make only legal moves to win, so, being rational, it restricts itself to these. Now rank the legal moves from best (wisest, most rational) to worst (stupidest, most self-defeating) and make your prediction: the computer will make the best move. You may well not be sure what the best move *is* (the computer may "appreciate" the situation better than you do!), but you can almost always eliminate all but four or five candidate moves, which still gives you tremendous predictive leverage.

Sometimes, when the computer finds itself in a tough predicament, with only one nonsuicidal move to make (a "forced" move), you can predict its move with supreme confidence. Nothing about the laws of physics forces this move, and nothing about the specific design of the computer forces this move. The move is forced by the overwhelmingly good *reasons* for making it and not any other move. Any chess player, constructed of whatever physical materials, would make it. Even a ghost or an angel would make it! You come up with your intentional-stance prediction on the basis of your bold assumption that *no matter how* the computer program has been designed, it has been designed well enough to be moved by such a good reason. You predict its behavior *as if* it were a rational agent.

The intentional stance is undeniably a useful shortcut in such a case, but how seriously should we take it? What does a computer care, really, about whether it wins or loses? Why say that the alarm clock *desires* to obey its master? We can use this contrast between natural and artificial goals to heighten our appreciation of the fact that all real goals ultimately spring from the predicament of a living, self-protective thing. But we must also recognize that the intentional stance *works* (when it does) whether or not the attributed goals are genuine or natural or "really appreciated" by the so-called agent, and this tolerance is crucial to understanding how genuine goal-seeking could be established in the first place. Does the macromolecule *really* want to replicate itself? The intentional stance explains what is going on, regardless of how we answer that question. Consider a simple organism—say, a planarian or an amoeba—moving nonrandomly across the bottom of a laboratory dish, always heading to the nutrient-rich end of the dish, or away from the toxic end. This organism is seeking the good, or shunning the bad—*its own* good and bad, not those of some human artifact-user. Seeking one's own good is a fundamental feature of any rational agent, but are these simple organisms seeking or just "seeking?" We don't need to answer that question. The organism is a predictable intentional system in either case.

This is another way of making Socrates' point in the *Meno*, when he asks whether anyone ever knowingly desires evil. We intentional systems do sometimes desire evil, through misunderstanding or misinformation or sheer lunacy, but it is part and parcel of rationality to desire what is deemed good. It is this constitutive relationship between the good and the seeking of the good that is endorsed—or rather enforced—by the natural selection of our forebears: those with the misfortune to be genetically designed so that they seek what is bad for them leave no descendants in the long run. It is no accident that the products of natural selection seek (or "seek") what they deem (or "deem") to be good.

Even the simplest organisms, if they are to favor what is good for them, need some sense organs or discriminative powers—some simple switches that turn ON in the presence of good and OFF in its absence—and these switches, or *transducers*, must be united to the right bodily responses. This requirement is the birth of *function*. A rock can't malfunction, for it has not been well- or ill-equipped to further any good. When we decide to interpret an entity from the intentional stance, it is as if we put ourselves in the role of its guardian, asking ourselves, in effect, "If *I* were in this organism's predicament, what would I do?" And here we expose the underlying anthropomorphism of the intentional stance: we treat all intentional systems as if they were just like us—which of course they are not.

Is this then a misapplication of our own perspective, the perspective *we mind-havers* share? Not necessarily. From the vantage point of evolutionary history, this is what has happened: Over billions of years, organisms gradually evolved, accumulating ever more versatile machinery designed to further their ever more complex and articulated goods. Eventually, with the evolution in our species of language and the varieties of reflectiveness that language permits (a topic for later chapters), we emerged with the ability to wonder the wonders with which we began this book—wonders about the minds of other entities. These wonders, naively conducted by our ancestors, led to *animism*, the idea that each moving thing has a mind or soul (*anima,* in Latin). We began to ask ourselves not only whether the tiger wanted to eat us—which it probably did—but why the rivers wanted to reach the seas, and what the clouds wanted from us in return for the rain we asked of them. As we became more sophisticated—and this is a very recent historical development, not anything to be discerned in the vast reaches of evolutionary time—we gradually withdrew the intentional stance from what we now call *inanimate* nature, reserving it for things more like us: animals, in the main, but also plants under many conditions. We still "trick" flowers into blooming prematurely by "deceiving" them with artificial spring warmth and light, and "encourage" vegetables to send down longer roots by withholding from them the water they want so badly. (A logger once explained to me how he knew we would find no white pines among the trees in some high ground in my forest—"Pines like to keep their feet wet.") This way of thinking about plants is not only natural and harmless but positively an aid to comprehension and an important lever for discovery. When biologists discover that a plant has some rudimentary discriminatory organ, they immediately ask themselves what the organ is for—what devious project does the plant have that requires it to obtain information from its environment on this topic? Very often the answer is an important scientific discovery.

Intentional systems are, by definition, all and only those entities whose behavior is predictable/explicable from the intentional stance. Self-replicating macromolecules, thermostats, amoebas, plants, rats, bats, people, and chess-playing computers are all intentional systems—some much more interesting than others. Since the point of the intentional stance is to treat an entity as an agent in order to predict its actions, we have to suppose that it is a smart agent, since a stupid agent might do any dumb thing at all. This bold leap of supposing that the agent will make only the smart moves (given its limited perspective) is what gives us the leverage to make predictions. We describe that limited perspective by attributing *particular* beliefs and desires to the agent on the basis of its perception of the situation and its goals or needs. Since our predictive leverage in this exercise is critically dependent on this particularity—since it is sensitive to the particular way the beliefs and desires are expressed by us, the theorists, or represented by the intentional system in question, I call such systems *intentional* systems. They exhibit what philosophers call *intentionality*.

"Intentionality," in this special philosophical sense, is such a controversial concept, and is so routinely misunderstood and misused by nonphilosophers, that I must pause to belabor its definition. Unfortunately for interdisciplinary communication, the philosophical term "intentionality" has two false friends—perfectly good words that are readily confused with it, and indeed are rather closely related to it. One is an ordinary term, the other is technical (and I will postpone its introduction briefly). In ordinary parlance, we often discuss whether someone's action was intentional or not. When the driver crashed into the bridge abutment, was he intentionally committing suicide, or had he fallen asleep? When you called the policeman "Dad" just then, was that intentional, or a slip of the tongue? Here we are asking, are we not, about the intentionality of the two deeds? Yes, in the ordinary sense; no, in the philosophical sense.

Intentionality in the philosophical sense is just *aboutness*. Something exhibits intentionality if its competence is in some way *about* something else. An alternative would be to say that something that exhibits intentionality contains a *representation* of something else—but I find that less revealing and more problematic. Does a lock contain a representation of the key that opens it? A lock and key exhibit the crudest form of intentionality; so do the opioid receptors in brain cells—receptors that are designed to accept the endorphin molecules that nature has been providing in brains for millions of years. Both can be tricked—that is, opened by an impostor. Morphine molecules are artifactual skeleton keys that have recently been fashioned to open the opioid-receptor doors too. (In fact it was the discovery of these highly specific receptors which inspired the search that led to the discovery of endorphins, the brain's own painkillers. There must have been something already present in the brain, reasearchers reasoned, for these specialized receptors to have been *about* in the first place.) This lock-and-key variety of crude aboutness is the basic design element out of which nature has fashioned the fancier sorts of subsystems that may more deservedly be called representation systems, so we will have to analyze the aboutness of these representations in terms of the (quasi?) aboutness of locks-and-keys in any case. We can stretch a point and say that the present shape of the bimetallic spring in a thermostat is a representation of the present room temperature, and that the position of the thermostat's adjustable lever is a representation of the desired room temperature, but we can equally well deny that these are, properly speaking, representations. They do, however, embody information *about* room temperature, and it is by virtue of that embodiment that they contribute to the competence of a simple intentional system.

Why do philosophers call aboutness "intentionality"? It all goes back to the medieval philosophers who coined the term, noting the similarity between such phenomena and the act of aiming an arrow at something (*intendere arcum in*). Intentional phenomena are equipped with metaphorical arrows, you might say, aimed at something or other—at whatever it is the phenomena are about or refer to or allude to. But of course many phenomena that exhibit this minimal sort of intentionality do not do anything *intentionally,* in the everyday sense of the term. Perceptual states, emotional states, and states of memory, for example, all exhibit aboutness without necessarily being intentional in the ordinary sense; they can be entirely involuntary or automatic responses to one thing or another. There is nothing intentional about recognizing a horse when it looms into view, but your state of recognition exhibits very particular aboutness: you recognize it *as* a horse. If you had misperceived it *as* a moose or a man on a motorcycle, your perceptual state would have had a different aboutness. It would have aimed its arrow rather differently—at something nonexistent, in fact, but nevertheless quite definite: either the moose that never was, or the illusory motorcyclist. There is a large psychological difference between mistakenly thinking you're in the presence of a moose and mistakenly thinking you're in the presence of a man on a motorcycle, a difference with predictable consequences. The medieval theorists noted that the arrow of intentionality could thus be aimed at nothing while nevertheless being aimed in a rather particular way. They called the object of your thought, real or not, the *intentional object*.

In order to think about something, you must have a way—one way among many possible ways—of thinking about it. Any intentional system is dependent on its particular ways of thinking about—perceiving, searching for, identifying, fearing, recalling—whatever it is that its "thoughts" are about. It is this dependency that creates all the opportunities for confusion, both practical and theoretical. Practically, the best way to confuse a particular intentional system is to exploit a flaw in its way(s) of perceiving or thinking about whatever it needs to think about. Nature has explored countless variations on this theme, since confusing other intentional systems is a major goal in the life of most intentional systems. After all, one of the primary desires of any living intentional system is the desire for the food needed to fuel growth, self-repair, and reproduction, so every living thing needs to distinguish the food (the good material) from the rest of the world. It follows that another primary desire is to avoid becoming the food of another intentional system. So camouflage, mimicry, stealth, and a host of other stratagems have put nature's locksmiths to the test, provoking the evolution of ever more effective ways of distinguishing one thing from another and keeping track of them. But no way is ever foolproof. There is no *taking* without the possibility of *mistaking*. That's why it's so important for us as theorists to be able to identify and distinguish the different varieties of taking (and mistaking) that can occur in intentional systems. In order to make sense of a system's actual "take" on its circumstances, we have to have an accurate picture of its dependence on its particular capacities for distinguishing things—its ways of "thinking about" things.

Unfortunately, however, as theorists we have tended to overdo it, treating *our own* well-nigh limitless capacity for distinguishing one thing from another in our thoughts (thanks to our ability to use language) as if it were the hallmark of all genuine intentionality, all aboutness worthy of the name. For instance, when a frog's tongue darts out and catches whatever is flying by, the frog may make a mistake—it may ingest a ball bearing thrown by a mischievous child, or a fisherman's lure on a monofilament thread, or some other inedible anomaly. The frog has made a mistake, but *exactly* which mistake(s) has it made? What did the frog "think" it was grabbing? A fly? Airborne food? A moving dark convexity? We language users can draw indefinitely fine distinctions of content for the candidate frog-thought, and there has been an unexamined assumption that before we can attribute any *real* intentionality to the frog we have to narrow down the content of the frog's states and acts with the same precision we can use (in principle) when we consider human thoughts and their propositional content.

This has been a major source of theoretical confusion, and to make matters worse, there is a handy technical term from logic that refers to just this capacity of language for making indefinitely fine-grained discriminations: *intensionality*. With an *s*. Intensionality-with-an-s is a feature of languages; it has no direct application to any other sort of representational system (pictures, maps, graphs, "search images," . . . minds). According to standard usage among logicians, the words or symbols in a language can be divided into the logical, or function, words ("if," "and," "or," "not," "all," "some," . . .) and the *terms* or *predicates*, which can be as various as the topic of discussion ("red," "tall," "grandfather," "oxygen," "second-rate composer of sonnets," . . .). Every meaningful term or predicate of a language has an *extension*—the thing or set of things to which the term refers—and an *intension*—the particular way in which this thing or set of things is picked out or determined. "Chelsea Clinton's father" and "president of the United States in 1995" name the very same thing—Bill Clinton—and hence have the same extension, but they zero in on this common entity in different ways, and hence have difference intensions. The term "equilateral triangle" picks out exactly the same set of things as the term "equiangular triangle," so these two terms have the same extension, but clearly they don't mean the same thing: one term is *about* a triangle's sides being equal and the other is *about* the angles being equal. So intension (with an s) is contrasted to extension, and means, well, *meaning*. And isn't that what intentionality-with-a-t means, too?

For many purposes, logicians note, we can ignore differences in the *intensions* of terms and just keep track of *extensions*. After all, a rose by any other name would smell as sweet, so if roses are the topic, the indefinitely many different ways of getting the class of roses into the discussion should be equivalent, from a logical point of view. Since water *is* H_2O, anything truly said of water, using the term "water," will be just as truly said if we substitute the term "H_2O" in its place—even if these two terms are subtly different in meaning, or intension. This freedom is particularly obvious and useful in such topic areas as mathematics, where you can always avail yourself of the practice of "substituting equals for equals," replacing "4^2" by "16" or vice versa, since these two different terms refer to one and the same number. Such freedom of substitution within linguistic contexts is aptly called *referential transparency*: you can see right through the terms, in effect, to the things the terms refer to. But when the topic is not roses but *thinking-about-roses*, or *talking-about-(thinking-about)-roses*, differences in intension can matter. So whenever the topic is intentional systems and their beliefs and desires, the language used by the theorist is intension-sensitive. A logician would say that such discourse exhibits *referential opacity*; it is not transparent; the terms themselves get in the way and interfere in subtle and confusing ways with the topic.

To see how referential opacity actually matters when we adopt the intentional stance, let's consider a root case of the intentional stance in action, applied to a human being. We do this effortlessly every day, and seldom spell out what is involved, but here is an example, drawn from a recent philosophical article—an example that goes rather weirdly but usefully into more detail than usual:

> Brutus wanted to kill Caesar. He believed that Caesar was an ordinary mortal, and that, given this, stabbing him (by which we mean plunging a knife into his heart) was a way of killing him. He thought that he could stab Caesar, for he remembered that he had a knife and saw that Caesar was standing next to him on his left in the Forum. So Brutus was motivated to stab the man to his left. He did so, thereby killing Caesar. (Israel, Perry, and Tutiya, 1993. p. 515)

Notice that the term "Caesar" is surreptitiously playing a crucial double role in this explanation—not just in the normal, transparent way of picking out a man, Caesar, the chap in the toga standing in the Forum, but in picking out the man *in the way Brutus himself picks him out*. It is not enough for Brutus to see Caesar standing next to him; he has to see that he *is* Caesar, the man he wants to kill. If Brutus mistook Caesar, the man to his left, for Cassius, then he wouldn't try to kill him: he wouldn't have been motivated, as the authors say, to stab the man to his left, since he would not have drawn the crucial connection in his mind—the link identifying the man to his left with his goal.

THE MISGUIDED GOAL OF
PROPOSITIONAL PRECISION
········

Whenever an agent acts, it acts on the basis of a particular understanding—or misunderstanding—of the circumstances, and intentional explanations and predictions rely on capturing that understanding. To predict the action of an intentional system, you have to know what things the beliefs and desires of the agent are about, *and* you have to know, at least roughly, *how* those beliefs and desires are about those things, so you can say whether the crucial connections have been, or will be, drawn.

But notice that I said that when we adopt the intentional stance we have to know *at least roughly* how the agent picks out the objects of concern. Failing to notice this is a major source of confusion. We typically don't need to know *exactly* what way the agent conceives of his task. The intentional stance can usually tolerate a lot of slack, and that's a blessing, since the task of expressing *exactly* how the agent conceives of his task is misconceived, as pointless an exercise as reading poems in a book through a microscope. If the agent under examination doesn't conceive of its circumstances with the aid of a language capable of making certain distinctions, the superb resolving power of our language can't be harnessed directly to the task of *expressing* the particular thoughts, or ways of thinking, or varieties of sensitivity, of that agent. (Indirectly, however, language can be used to *describe* those particularities in whatever detail the theoretical context demands.)

This point often gets lost in the mists of a spuriously persuasive argument, along the following lines. Do dogs (for example) think? If so, then of course they must think particular thoughts. A thought couldn't exist without being some particular thought or other, could it? But a particular thought must be composed of particular concepts. You can't think the thought

>   *that my dish is full of beef*

unless you have the concepts of *dish* and *beef*, and to have these concepts you have to have a host of other concepts (*bucket, plate, cow, flesh, . . .*), since this particular thought is readily distinguishable (by us) from the thought

>   *that the bucket is full of beef*

as well as from the thought

>   *that my plate is full of calves' liver*

to say nothing of the thought

>   *that the red, tasty stuff in the thing that I usually eat from is not the usual dry stuff they feed me*

and so on and so forth, forever. Just which thought or thoughts is the dog thinking? How can we express—in English, say—exactly the thought the dog is thinking? If it can't be done (and it can't), then either dogs can't think thoughts at all or dogs' thoughts must be systematically inexpressible—and hence beyond our ken.

Neither alternative follows. The idea that a dog's "thought" might be inexpressible (in human language) for the simple reason that expression in a human language *cuts too fine* is often ignored, along with its corollary: the idea that we may nevertheless exhaustively describe what we can't express, leaving no mysterious residue at all. The dog has to have its particular ways of discriminating things, and these ways get composed into quite particular and idiosyn-cratic "concepts." If we can figure out how these ways work, and describe how they work together, then we will know as much about the content of the dog's thoughts as we ever learn about the content of another human being's thoughts through conversation, even if we can't find a sentence (in English or in any other human language) that *expresses* that content.

When we human mind-havers, from our uniquely ele-vated perspective, use *our* special trick of applying the intentional stance to other entities, we are imposing our ways on them, and we risk importing too much clarity, too much distinctness and articulation of content, and hence too much organization, to the systems we are attempting to understand. We also risk importing too much of the particu-lar *kind* of organization of our own minds to our model of these simpler systems. Not all of our needs, and hence desires, and hence mental practices, and hence mental resources, are shared by these simpler candidates for minds.

Many organisms "experience" the sun, and even guide their lives by its passage. A sunflower may track the sun in a minimal way, twisting to face it as it crosses the sky, maxi-mizing its daily exposure to sunlight, but it can't cope with an intervening umbrella. It can't anticipate the sun's reemer-gence at a calculable later time and adjust its slow, simple "behavior" accordingly. An animal might well be capable of such sophistication, modulating its locomotion to keep itself hidden in shadows from its prey, or even anticipating where to stretch out in the sun for a long nap, appreciating (dimly and unthinkingly) that the tree's shadow will soon lengthen. Animals track and reidentify other things (mates, quarry, off-spring, favorite food sites), and they might similarly track the sun. But we human beings don't just track the sun, we make an ontological discovery about the sun: it's *the sun*! The very same sun each day.

The German logician Gottlob Frege introduced an example that logicians and philosophers have written about for more than a century: the Morning Star, known to the ancients as Phosphorus, and the Evening Star, known to the ancients as Hesperus, are one and the same heavenly body: Venus. Today this is a familiar fact, but the discovery of this identity was a substantial early advance in astronomy. Which of us today could formulate the argument and amass the crucial evidence without looking for help in a book? Even as small children, we readily understand (and docilely accept) the hypothesis, however. It's hard to imagine that any other creatures could ever be brought to formulate, much less confirm, the hypothesis that these small bright spots are one and the same heavenly body.

Couldn't those huge, hot disks that make a daily passage across the skies be new every day? We're the only species that can even formulate the question. Compare sun and moon to the seasons. Spring comes back each year, but we don't ask (any more) if it's the *same* spring, returned. Perhaps Spring, personified as a goddess in the old days, *was* seen by our ancestors as a returning particular, not a recurring universal. But for other species this isn't even an issue. Some species have exquisite sensitivity to variations; they can discriminate many more details, in some domains, than we can with our naked senses (although as far as we know, we can, with the aid of our prosthetic extensions—microscopes, spectroscopes, gas chromatographs, and so forth—make finer discriminations in every single modality than any other creatures on the planet). But these other species have a very limited ability to reflect, and their sensitivities are channeled down rather narrow sets of possibilities, as we shall see.

We, in contrast, are *believe-alls*. There is no limit, apparently, to what we can believe, and to what we can distinguish in belief. We can distinguish between believing

> *that the sun is and always has been the same star, each day,*

and believing

> *that the sun has been the same star, each day, since January 1, 1900, when the latest sun took over its role from its predecessor.*

I take it that nobody believes the latter, but it is easy enough to see what the belief is, and to distinguish it both from the standard belief and from the equally daft but different belief,

> *that the most recent change of suns happened on June 12, 1986.*

The fundamental form of all such attributions of mental states to intentional systems are sentences that express what are called *propositional attitudes*.

> x believes that p.
> y desires that q.
> z wonders whether r.

Such sentences consist of three parts: a term referring to the intentional system in question (x, y, z), a term for the attitude attributed to it (belief, desire, wonder, . . .), and a term for the particular content or meaning of that attitude—the *proposition* denoted in these dummy cases by the letters p, q, and r. In actual attribution sentences, of course, these propositions are *expressed* as *sentences* (of English, or whatever language the speaker is using), and these sentences contain terms that may not be substituted ad lib for coextensive terms—that's the feature of referential opacity.

Propositions, then, are the theoretical entities with which

we identify, or measure, beliefs. For two believers to share a belief is, by definition, for them to believe one and the same proposition. What then are propositions? They are, by mutually agreed philosophical convention, the abstract meanings shared by all *sentences* that . . . mean the same thing. An ominous circle emerges from the smoke of battle. Presumably, one and the same proposition is expressed by

1. Snow is white.
2. La neige est blanche.
3. Der Schnee ist weiss.

After all, when I attribute to Tom the belief that snow is white, we want Pierre and Wilhelm to be able to attribute the same belief to Tom in their own tongues. The fact that Tom need not understand their attributions is beside the point. For that matter, Tom need not understand *my* attribution, of course, since perhaps Tom is a cat, or a monolingual Turk.

But is one and the same proposition also shared by the following?

4. Bill hit Sam.
5. Sam was hit by Bill.
6. It was Bill who was the agent of the act of hitting of which Sam was the victim.

They all "say the same thing," and yet they all say "it" in different ways. Should propositions line up with *ways of saying* or with *things said*? A simple, theoretically appealing way of settling the issue would be to ask whether a believer can believe one of these without believing another. If so, then they are different propositions. After all, if propositions are to be the theoretical entities that measure belief, we wouldn't want this test to fail. But how can we test this if Tom isn't an English speaker, or a speaker at all? We attributors—at least when we express our attributions in language—must be bound by a system of expression, a language, and languages differ in their structures as well as their terms. By being forced into one such language structure or another, we willy-nilly take on more distinctions than the circumstances may warrant. This is the point of the warning I issued earlier about the *rough* attribution of content that suffices for the success of the intentional stance.

The philosopher Paul Churchland (1979) has likened propositions to numbers—equally abstract objects used to measure many physical properties.

x has weight-in-grams of *144*.
y has speed-in-meters-per-second of *12*.

Obviously, numbers are well-behaved occupants of this role. We can "substitute equals for equals." There is no difficulty in agreeing that *x* has weight-in-grams of *2×72* or that *y* has speed-in-meters-per-second of *9+3*. There is a difficulty, as we have just seen, when we try to apply the same rules of transformation and equivalence to different expressions of what are putatively the same proposition. Propositions, alas, are not as well-behaved theoretical entities as numbers. Propositions are more like dollars than numbers!

This goat is worth *$50*.

And how much is it worth in Greek drachmas, or Russian rubles (on what day of the week!)—and is it worth more or less today than it was in ancient Athens or as part of Marco Polo's expeditionary supplies? There is no doubt that a goat always has a value to its owner, and there is no doubt that we can fix a rough, operational measure of its value by executing—or imagining ourselves to execute—an exchange for money, or gold dust, or bread, or whatever. But there is no fixed, neutral, eternal system of measuring economic value, and likewise there is no fixed, neutral, eternal system for measuring meaning by the propositionful. So what? It would be nice, I guess, if there were such systems; it would make for a neater world, and it might make the theoretician's job simpler. But such a single-standard, universal system of measurement is unnecessary for theory in both economics and intentional-system theory. Sound economic theory is not threatened by the ineliminable imprecision in its measurement of economic value generalized to all circumstances at all times. Sound intentional-system theory is not threatened by the ineliminable imprecision in its measurement of meaning across the same universal spectrum. As long as we are alert to the difficulty, we can deal with all local problems quite satisfactorily, using whatever rough-and-ready system we choose.

In subsequent chapters, we will find that when we take our "believe-all" competence and apply it to "lower" creatures, it handily organizes the data for us: it tells us where to look next, sets boundary conditions, and highlights patterns of similarity and difference. But if we are not careful, as we have already seen, it can also woefully distort our vision. It is one thing to treat an organism, or any of its many subsystems, as a rudimentary intentional system that crudely and *unthinkingly* pursues its undeniably sophisticated ends, and quite another to impute reflective appreciation to it of what it is doing. Our kind of reflective thinking is a very recent evolutionary innovation.

The original self-replicating macromolecules *had* reasons for what they did, but had no inkling of them. We, in contrast, not only know—or think we know—our reasons; we articulate them, discuss them, criticize them, share them. They are not just the reasons we act; they are reasons *for us*. In between the macromolecules and us there is quite a story to be told. Consider, for instance, the fledgling cuckoo, hatched in an alien nest by unwitting adoptive parents. Its first action when it emerges from its egg is to roll the other eggs out of the nest. This is not an easy task, and it is quite astonishing to watch the ferocious single-mindedness and resourcefulness with which the baby bird overcomes whatever obstacles lie in its way to jettison the other eggs. Why does it do this? Because those eggs contain rivals for the attentions of its surrogate providers. By disposing of these rivals, it maximizes the food and protective care it will receive. The newborn cuckoo is, of course, oblivious; it has no inkling of this rationale for its ruthless act, but the rationale is *there*, and has undoubtedly shaped this innate behavior over the eons. *We* can see it, even if the cuckoo can't. I call such a rationale "free floating," because it is nowhere *represented* in the fledgling, or anywhere else, even though it is operative—over evolutionary time—in shaping and refining the behavior in question (in providing for its informational needs, for instance). The strategic principles involved are not explicitly encoded but just implicit in the larger organization of designed features. How did those reasons get captured and articulated in some of the minds that have evolved? That's a good question. It will occupy our attention for several chapters, but before going on to consider it, I must address a residual suspicion some philosophers have aired, to wit: I have it exactly backward. I am proposing to explain real intentionality in terms of pseudo-intentionality! Moreover, it seems, I am failing to acknowledge the important distinction between *original* or *intrinsic* intentionality and *derived* intentionality. What is the distinction?

ORIGINAL AND DERIVED INTENTIONALITY
········

According to some philosophers, following John Searle (1980), intentionality comes in two varieties, intrinsic (or original) and derived. Intrinsic intentionality is the aboutness of our thoughts, our beliefs, our desires, our intentions (intentions in the ordinary sense). It is the obvious *source* of the distinctly limited and derived sort of aboutness exhibited by some of our artifacts: our words, sentences, books, maps, pictures, computer programs. They have intentionality only by courtesy of a kind of generous loan from our minds. The derived intentionality of our artifactual representations is parasitic on the genuine, original, intrinsic intentionality that lies behind their creation.

There is a lot to be said for this claim. If you close your eyes and think about Paris, or your mother, that thought of yours is about its object in the most primary and direct way that anything could be about anything. If you then write a description of Paris, or draw a sketch of your mother, the representation on the paper is about Paris, or your mother, only because that is your authorial intention (ordinary sense). You are in charge of your representations, and you get to declare or decide what these creations of yours are about. There are conventions of language that you rely on to assist in this injection of meaning into brute marks on paper. Unless you have just previously declared that henceforth you shall mean to refer to Boston whenever you say or write the word "Paris" or that you choose to call Michelle Pfeiffer "Mother," the standard references agreed to by your linguistic community are assumed to be in force. These conventions, in turn, depend on the communal intentions of that community. So external representations get their meanings—their intensions and extensions—from the meanings of the internal, mental states and acts of the people who make them and use them. Those mental states and acts have original intentionality.

The point about the dependent status of artifactual representations is undeniable. Manifestly, the pencil marks in themselves don't mean a thing. This is particularly clear in cases of ambiguous sentences. The philosopher W. V. O. Quine gives us the nice example:

Our mothers bore us.

What is this thing *about*? Is this a present-tense complaint about boredom or a past-tense truism about our origins? You have to ask the person who created the sentence. Nothing about the marks in themselves could possibly determine the answer. *They* certainly don't have intrinsic intentionality, whatever that might be. If they mean anything at all, it is because of the role they play in a system of representation that is anchored to the minds of the representers.

But what of the states and acts of those minds? What endows them with their intentionality? One popular answer is to say that these mental states and acts have meaning because they themselves, marvelously enough, are composed in a sort of language—the language of thought. Mentalese. This is a hopeless answer. It is hopeless not because there couldn't be any such system to be found in the internal goings-on in people's brains. Indeed, there could be—though any such system wouldn't be *just* like an ordinary natural language, such as English or French. It is hopeless as an answer to the question we posed, for it merely postpones the question. Let there be a language of thought. Now whence comes the meaning of *its* terms? How do you know what the sentences in your language of thought mean? This problem comes into sharper focus if we contrast the language-of-thought hypothesis with its ancestor and chief rival, the picture theory of ideas. Our thoughts are like pictures, runs this view; they are about what they are about because, like pictures, they *resemble* their objects. How do I tell my idea of a duck from my idea of a cow? By noting that my idea of a duck *looks like a duck*, while my idea of a cow doesn't! This, too, is hopeless, because it immediately raises the question, And how do you know what a duck looks like? Again, it's not hopeless because there couldn't be a system of imagery in your brain that exploits pictorial resemblances between the brain's internal images and the things they represent; indeed, there could be. In fact, there is, and we are beginning to understand how such a system works. It is hopeless as an answer to our basic question, however, because it depends on the very understanding that it's supposed to explain, and hence goes round in circles.

The solution to this problem of our intentionality is straightforward. We just agreed that representational artifacts (such as written descriptions and sketches) possess derived intentionality, by virtue of the role they play in the activities of their creators. A shopping list written down on a piece of paper has only the derived intentionality it gets from the intentions of the agent who made it. Well, so does a shopping list held by the same agent in memory! Its intentionality is exactly as derived as that of the external list, and for the same reasons. Similarly, a merely mental image of your mother—or Michelle Pfeiffer—is about its object in just as derived a way as the sketch you draw. It is internal, not external, but it is still an artifact created by your brain and means what it does because of its particular position in the ongoing economy of your brain's internal activities and their role in governing your body's complex activities in the real, surrounding world.

And how did your brain come to have an organization of such amazing states with such amazing powers? Play the same card again: the brain is an artifact, and it gets whatever intentionality its parts have from their role in the ongoing economy of the larger system of which it is a part—or, in other words, from the intentions of its creator, Mother Nature (otherwise known as the process of evolution by natural selection).

This idea that the intentionality of brain states is derived from the intentionality of the system or process that designed them is admittedly a strange and unsettling idea, at first. We can see what it comes to by considering a context in which it is surely correct: When we wonder about the (derived) intentionality of the "brain" states of some manufactured robot. Suppose we come across a robot trundling a shopping cart through a supermarket and periodically consulting a slip of paper with symbols written on it. One line is:

MILK@.5×GAL if P<2×QT\P else 2×MILK@QT

What, if anything, is this gibberish *about*? We ask the robot. It replies, "That's just to remind me to get a half gallon of milk, but only if the price of a half gallon is less than twice the price of a quart. Quarts are easier for me to carry." This auditory artifact emitted by the robot is mainly just a translation into English of the written one, but it wears *its* derived meaning on its sleeve, for our benefit. And where did either of these artifacts get their derived intentionality? From the clever engineering work of the robot's designers, no doubt, but maybe very indirectly. Maybe these engineers formulated and directly installed the cost-conscious principle that has spawned this particular reminder—a rather boring possibility, but one in which the derived intentionality of these states would definitely lead back to the human designers' own intentionality as the creators of those states. It would be much more interesting if the designers had done something deeper. It is possible—just on the edge of technological capability today—that they designed the robot to be cost-sensitive in many ways and let it "figure out," from its own "experience," that it should adopt some such principle. In this case, the principle would not be hard-wired but flexible, and in the near future the robot might decide from its further "experience" that this application was not cost-effective after all, and it would buy milk in convenient quarts no matter what they cost. How much design work did the robot's designers do, and how much did they delegate to the robot itself? The more elaborate the system of controls, with its attendant information-gathering and information-assessing subsystems, the greater the contribution of the robot itself, and hence the greater its claim to be the "author" of its own meanings—meanings that might, over time, become quite inscrutable to the robot's designers.

The imagined robot does not yet exist, but someday it might. I introduce it in order to show that *within* its world of merely derived intentionality we can draw the very distinction that inspired the contrast between original and derived intentionality in the first place. (We had to "consult the author" to discover the meaning of the artifact.) This is instructive, because it shows that derived intentionality can be derived from derived intentionality. It also shows how an illusion of intrinsic intentionality (*metaphysically* original intentionality) could arise. It might *seem* that the author of a puzzling artifact would have to have intrinsic intentionality in order to be the source of the artifact's derived intentionality, but this is not so. We can see that in this case, at least, there is no work left over for *intrinsic* intentionality to do. The imagined robot would be just as capable as we are of delegating derived intentionality to further artifacts. It gets around in the world, advancing its projects and avoiding harm, on the strength of its "merely" derived intentionality, the intentionality designed into it—first by its designers and then, as it acquires more information about its world, by its own processes of self-redesign. We may perhaps be in the same predicament, living our lives by the lights of our "merely" derived intentionality. What boon would intrinsic intentionality (whatever that is) provide for us that could not as well have been bequeathed to us, as evolution-designed artifacts? Perhaps we are chasing a will-of-the-wisp.

It's a good thing that this prospect has opened up for us, because the intentionality that allows us to speak and write and wonder all manner of wonders is undeniably a late and complex product of an evolutionary process that has the cruder sorts of intentionality—disparaged by Searle and others as "mere *as if* intentionality"—as both its ancestors and its contemporary components. We are descended from robots, and composed of robots, and all the intentionality we enjoy is derived from the more fundamental intentionality of these billions of crude intentional systems. I don't have it backward; I have it forward. That's the only promising direction to travel. But the journey lies ahead.

....

CHAPTER 3

THE BODY AND ITS MINDS

> In the distant future I see open fields for far
> more important researches. Psychology will be
> based on a new foundation, that of the neces-
> sary acquirement of each mental power and
> capacity by gradation. Light will be thrown on
> the origin of man and his history.
>
> Charles Darwin, *The Origin of Species*

FROM SENSITIVITY TO SENTIENCE?
....

At last, let's take the journey. Mother Nature—or, as we call
it today, the process of evolution by natural selection—has
no foresight at all, but has gradually built beings with foresight. The task of a mind is to produce future, as the poet
Paul Valéry once put it. A mind is fundamentally an antici-
pator, an expectation-generator. It mines the present for
clues, which it refines with the help of the materials it has
saved from the past, turning them into anticipations of the

57

future. And then it acts, rationally, on the basis of those hard-won anticipations.

Given the inescapable competition for materials in the world of living things, the task facing any organism can be considered to be one version or another of the childhood game of hide-and-seek. You seek what you need, and hide from those who need what you have. The earliest replicators, the macromolecules, had their needs and developed simple—*relatively* simple!—means of achieving them. Their seeking was just so much random walking, with a suitably configured grabber at the business end. When they bumped into the right things, they grabbed them. These seekers had no plan, no "search image," no representation of the sought-for items beyond the configuration of the grabbers. It was lock-and-key, and nothing more. Hence the macromolecule did not know it was seeking, and did not need to know.

The "need to know" principle is most famous in its application in the world of espionage, actual and fictional: No agent should be given any more information than he absolutely needs to know to perform his part of the project. Much the same principle has been honored for billions of years, and continues to be honored in a trillion ways, in the design of every living thing. The agents (or microagents or pseudoagents) of which a living thing is composed—like the secret agents of the CIA or KGB—are vouchsafed only the information they need in order to carry out their very limited specialized tasks. In espionage, the rationale is security; in nature, the rationale is economy. The cheapest, least intensively designed system will be "discovered" first by Mother Nature, and myopically selected.

It is important to recognize, by the way, that the cheapest design may well not be the most efficient, or the smallest. It may often be cheaper for Mother Nature to throw in—or leave in—lots of extra, nonfunctioning stuff, simply because such stuff gets created by the replication-and-development process and cannot be removed without exorbitant cost. It is now known that many mutations insert a code that simply "turns off" a gene without deleting it—a much cheaper move to make in genetic space. A parallel phenomenon in the world of human engineering occurs routinely in computer programming. When programmers improve a program (creating, say, WordWhizbang 7.0 to replace WordWhizbang 6.1), the standard practice is to create the new source code adjacent to the old code, simply by copying the old code and then editing or mutating the copy. Then, before running or compiling the new code, they "comment out" the old code— they don't erase it from the source code file but isolate the old version between special symbols that tell the computer to skip over the bracketed stuff when compiling or executing the program. The old instructions remain in the "genome," marked so that they are never "expressed" in the phenotype. It costs almost nothing to keep the old code along for the ride, and it might come in handy some day. Circumstances in the world might change, for instance—making the old version better after all. Or the extra copy of the old version might someday get mutated into something of value. Such hard-won design should not be lightly discarded, since it would be hard to re-create from scratch. As is becoming ever more clear, evolution often avails itself of this tactic, reusing again and again the leftovers of earlier design processes. (I explore this principle of thrifty accumulation of design in more depth in *Darwin's Dangerous Idea*.)

The macromolecules had no need to know, and their single-celled descendants were much more complex but also had no need to know what they were doing, or why what they were doing was the source of their livelihood. For billions of years, then, there were reasons but no reason formulators, or reason representers, or even, in the strong sense, reason appreciators. (Mother Nature, the process of natural selection, shows her appreciation of good reasons tacitly, by wordlessly and mindlessly permitting the best designs to prosper.) We late-blooming theorists are the first to *see* the patterns and divine these reasons—the free-floating rationales of the designs that have been created over the eons.

We describe the patterns using the intentional stance. Even some of the simplest design features in organisms— permanent features even simpler than ON/OFF switches— can be installed and refined by a process that has an intentional-stance interpretation. For instance, plants don't have minds by any stretch of the theorist's imagination, but over evolutionary time their features are shaped by competitions that can be modeled by mathematical game theory—it is *as if* the plants and their competitors were agents like us! Plants that have an evolutionary history of being heavily preyed upon by herbivores often evolve toxicity to those herbivores as a retaliatory measure. The herbivores, in turn, often evolve a specific tolerance in their digestive systems for those specific toxins, and return to the feast, until the day when the plants, foiled in their first attempt, develop further toxicity or prickly barbs, as their next move in an escalating arms race of measure and countermeasure. At some point, the herbivores may "choose" not to retaliate but rather to discriminate, turning to other food sources, and then other nontoxic plants may evolve to "mimic" the toxic plants, blindly exploiting a weakness in the discriminatory system—visual or olfactory—of the herbivores and thereby hitching a free ride on the toxicity defense of the other plant species. The free-floating rationale is clear and predictive, even though neither the plants nor the digestive systems of the herbivores have minds in anything like the ordinary sense.

All this happens at an achingly slow pace, by our standards. It can take thousands of generations, thousands of years, for a single move in this game of hide-and-seek to be made and responded to (though in some circumstances the pace is shockingly fast). The patterns of evolutionary change emerge so slowly that they are invisible at our normal rate of information uptake, so it's easy to overlook their intentional interpretation, or to dismiss it as mere whimsy or metaphor. This bias in favor of *our* normal pace might be called *timescale chauvinism*. Take the smartest, quickest-witted person you know, and imagine filming her in action in ultra-slow motion—say, thirty thousand frames per second, to be projected at the normal rate of thirty frames per second. A single lightning riposte, a witticism offered "without skipping a beat," would now emerge like a glacier from her mouth, boring even the most patient moviegoer. Who could divine the intelligence of her performance, an intelligence that would be unmistakable at normal speed? We are also charmed by mismatched timescales going in the other direction, as time-lapse photography has vividly demonstrated. To watch flowers growing, budding, and blooming in a few seconds, is to be drawn almost irresistibly into the intentional stance. See how that plant is striving upward, racing its neighbor for a favored place in the sun, defiantly thrusting its own leaves into the light, parrying the counterblows, ducking and weaving like a boxer! The very same patterns, projected at different speeds, can reveal or conceal the presence of a mind, or the absence of a mind—or so it seems. (Spatial scale also shows a powerful built-in bias; if gnats were the size of seagulls, more people would be sure they had minds, and if we had to look through microscopes to see the antics of otters, we would be less confident that they were fun-loving.)

In order for us to see things as mindful, they have to happen at the right pace, and when we do see something as mindful, we don't have much choice; the perception is almost irresistible. But is this just a fact about our bias as observers, or is it a fact about minds? What is the *actual* role of speed in the phenomenon of mind? Could there be minds, as real as any minds anywhere, that conducted their activities orders of magnitude slower than our minds do? Here is a reason for thinking that there could be: if our planet were visited by Martians who thought the same sorts of thoughts we do but thousands or millions of times faster than we do, we would seem to them to be about as stupid as trees, and they would be inclined to scoff at the hypothesis that we had minds. If they did, they would be wrong, wouldn't they—victims of their own timescale chauvinism. So if we want to deny that there could be a radically slow-thinking mind, we will have to find some grounds other than our preference for the human thought rate. What grounds might there be? Perhaps, you may think, there is a minimum speed for a mind, rather like the minimum escape velocity required to overcome gravity and leave the planet. For this idea to have any claim on our attention, let alone allegiance, we would need a theory that says why this should be. What could it be about running a system faster and faster that eventually would "break the mind barrier" and create a mind where before there was none? Does the friction of the moving parts create heat, which above a certain temperature leads to the transformation of something at the chemical level? And why would that make a mind? Is it like particles in an accelerator approaching the speed of light and becoming hugely massive? Why would that make a mind? Does the rapid spinning of the brain parts somehow weave a containment vessel to prevent the escape of the accumulating mind particles until a critical mass of them coheres into a mind? Unless something along these lines can be proposed *and defended*, the idea that sheer speed is essential for minds is unappealing, since there is such a good reason for holding that it's the *relative* speed that matters: perception, deliberation, and action all swift enough—relative to the unfolding environment—to accomplish the purposes of a mind. Producing future is no use to any intentional system if its "predictions" arrive too late to be acted on. Evolution will always favor the quick-witted over the slow-witted, other things being equal, and extinguish those who can't meet their deadlines well on a regular basis.

But what if there were a planet on which the speed of light was 100 kilometers per hour, and all other physical events and processes were slowed down to keep pace? Since in fact the pace of events in the physical world can't be sped up or slowed down by orders of magnitude (except in philosophers' fantastic thought experiments), a relative speed requirement works as well as an absolute speed requirement. Given the speed at which thrown stones approach their targets, and given the speed at which light bounces off those incoming stones, and given the speed at which audible warning calls can be propagated through the atmosphere, and given the force that must be marshaled to get 100 kilograms of body running at 20 kilometers per hour to veer sharply to the left or right—given these and a host of other firmly fixed performance specifications, useful brains have to operate at quite definite minimum speeds, independently of any fanciful "emergent properties" that might also be produced only at certain speeds. These speed-of-operation requirements, in turn, force brains to use media of information transmission that can sustain those speeds. That's one good reason why it can matter what a mind is made of. There may be others.

When the events in question unfold at a more stately pace, something mindlike can occur in other media. These patterns are discernible in these phenomena only when we adopt the intentional stance. Over very long periods of time, species or lineages of plants and animals can be *sensitive* to changing conditions, and *respond* to the changes they sense in rational ways. That's all it takes for the intentional stance to find predictive and explanatory leverage. Over much shorter periods of time, individual plants can respond appropriately to changes they sense in their environment, growing new leaves and branches to exploit the available sunlight, extending their roots toward water, and even (in some species) *temporarily* adjusting the chemical composition of their edible parts to ward off the *sensed onslaught* of transient herbivores.

These sorts of slow-paced sensitivity, like the artificial sensitivity of thermostats and computers, may strike us as mere second-rate imitations of the phenomenon that really makes the difference: *sentience*. Perhaps we can distinguish "mere intentional systems" from "genuine minds" by asking whether the candidates in question enjoy sentience. Well, what is it? "Sentience" has never been given a proper definition, but it is the more or less standard term for what is imagined to be the lowest grade of consciousness. We may wish to entertain the strategy, at about this point, of contrasting sentience with mere sensitivity, a phenomenon exhibited by single-celled organisms, plants, the fuel gauge in your car, and the film in your camera. Sensitivity need not involve consciousness at all. Photographic film comes in different grades of sensitivity to light; thermometers are made of materials that are sensitive to changes in temperature; litmus paper is sensitive to the presence of acid. Popular opinion proclaims that plants and perhaps "lower" animals—jellyfish, sponges, and the like—are sensitive without being sentient, but that "higher" animals are sentient. Like us, they are not *merely* endowed with sensitive equipment of one sort or another—equipment that responds differentially and appropriately to one thing or another. They enjoy some further property, called sentience—so says popular opinion. But what is this commonly proclaimed property?

What does sentience amount to, above and beyond sensitivity? This is a question that is seldom asked and has never been properly answered. We shouldn't assume that there's a good answer. We shouldn't assume, in other words, that it's a good question. If we want to use the concept of sentience, we will have to construct it from parts we understand. Everybody agrees that sentience requires sensitivity plus some further as yet unidentified factor x, so if we direct our attention to the different varieties of sensitivity and the roles in which they are exploited, keeping a sharp lookout for something that strikes us as a crucial addition, we may discover sentience along the way. Then we can add the phenomenon of sentience to our unfolding story—or, alternatively, the whole idea of sentience as a special category may evaporate. One way or another, we will cover the ground that separates conscious us from the merely sensitive, insentient macromolecules we are descended from. One tempting place to look for the key difference between sensitivity and sentience is in the materials involved—the *media* in which information travels and is transformed.

THE MEDIA AND THE MESSAGES
········

We must look more closely at the development I sketched at the beginning of chapter 2. The earliest control systems were really just body protectors. Plants are alive, but they don't have brains. They don't need them, given their lifestyle. They do, however, need to keep their bodies intact and properly situated to benefit from the immediate surroundings, and for this they evolved systems of self-governance or control that took account of the crucial variables and reacted accordingly. Their concerns—and hence their rudimentary intentionality—was either directed inward, to internal conditions, or directed to conditions at the all-important boundaries between the body and the cruel world. The responsibility for monitoring and making adjustments was distributed, not centralized. Local sensing of changing conditions could be met by local reactions, which were largely independent of each other. This could sometimes lead to coordination problems, with one team of microagents acting at cross-purposes to another. There are times when independent decision making is a bad idea; if everybody decides to lean to the right when the boat tips to the left, the boat may well tip over to the right. But in the main, the minimalist strategies of plants can be well met by highly distributed "decision making," modestly coordinated by the slow, rudimentary exchange of information by diffusion in the fluids coursing through the plant body.

Might plants then just be "very slow animals," enjoying sentience that has been overlooked by us because of our timescale chauvinism? Since there is no established meaning to the word "sentience," we are free to adopt one of our own choosing, if we can motivate it. We could refer to the slow but reliable responsiveness of plants to their environment as "sentience" if we wanted, but we would need some reason to distinguish this quality from the mere sensitivity exhibited by bacteria and other single-celled life-forms (to say nothing of light meters in cameras). There's no ready candidate for such a reason, and there's a fairly compelling reason for reserving the term "sentience" for something more special: animals have slow body-maintenance systems rather like those of plants, and common opinion differentiates between the operation of these systems and an animal's sentience.

Animals have had slow systems of body maintenance for as long as there have been animals. Some of the molecules floating along in such media as the bloodstream are themselves *operatives* that directly "do things" for the body (for instance, some of them destroy toxic invaders in one-on-one combat), and some are more like *messengers*, whose arrival at and "recognition" by some larger agent tells the larger agent to "do things" (for instance, to speed up the heart rate or initiate vomiting). Sometimes the larger agent is the entire body. For instance, when the pineal gland in some species detects a general decrease in daily sunlight, it broadcasts to the whole body a hormonal message to begin preparing for winter—a task with many subtasks, all set into motion by one message. Although activity in these ancient hormonal systems may be accompanied by powerful instances of what we may presume to be sentience (such as waves of nausea, or dizzy feelings, or chills, or pangs of lust), these systems operate independently of those sentient accompaniments— for instance, in sleeping or comatose animals. Doctors speak of brain-dead human beings kept alive on respirators as being in a "vegetative state," when these body-maintenance systems alone are keeping life and limb together. Sentience is gone, but sensitivity of many sorts persists, maintaining various bodily balances. Or at least that's how many people would want to apply these two words.

In animals, this complex system of biochemical packets of control information was eventually supplemented by a swifter system, running in a different medium: traveling pulses of electrical activity in nerve fibers. This opened up a space of opportunities for swifter reactions, but also permitted the control to be differently distributed, because of the different geometries of connection possible in this new system, the autonomic nervous system. The concerns of the new system were still internal—or, at any rate, immediate in both space and time: Should the body shiver now, or should it sweat? Should the digestive processes in the stomach be postponed because of more pressing needs for the blood supply? Should the countdown to ejaculation begin? And so forth. The interfaces between the new medium and the old had to be worked out by evolution, and the history of that development has left its marks on our current arrangements, making them much more complicated than one might have expected. Ignoring these complexities has often led theorists of mind astray—myself included—so we should note them, briefly.

One of the fundamental assumptions shared by many modern theories of mind is known as *functionalism*. The basic idea is well known in everyday life and has many proverbial expressions, such as *handsome is as handsome does*. What makes something a mind (or a belief, or a pain, or a fear) is not what it is made of, but what it *can do*. We appreciate this principle as uncontroversial in other areas, especially in our assessment of artifacts. What makes something a spark plug is that it can be plugged into a particular situation and *deliver a spark when called upon*. That's all that matters; its color or material or internal complexity can vary ad lib, and so can its shape, as long as its shape permits it to meet the specific dimensions of its functional role. In the world of living things, functionalism is widely appreciated: a heart is something for pumping blood, and an artificial heart or a pig's heart may do just about as well, and hence can be substituted for a diseased heart in a human body. There are more than a hundred chemically different varieties of the valuable protein lysozyme. What makes them all instances of lysozyme is what makes them valuable: what they can do. They are interchangeable, for almost all intents and purposes.

In the standard jargon of functionalism, these functionally defined entities admit *multiple realizations*. Why couldn't artificial minds, like artificial hearts, be made real—realized—out of almost anything? Once we figure out what minds do (what pains do, what beliefs do, and so on), we ought to be able to make minds (or mind parts) out of alternative materials that have those competences. And it has seemed obvious to many theorists—myself included— that what minds do is *process information*; minds are the control systems of bodies, and in order to execute their appointed duties they need to gather, discriminate, store, transform, and otherwise process information about the control tasks they perform. So far, so good. Functionalism, here as elsewhere, promises to make life easier for the theorist by abstracting away from some of the messy particularities of performance and focusing on the work that is actually getting done. But it's almost standard for functionalists to oversimplify their conception of this task, making life *too* easy for the theorist.

It's tempting to think of a nervous system (either an autonomic nervous system or its later companion, a central nervous system) as an information network tied at various specific places—transducer (or *input*) nodes and effector (or *output*) nodes—to the realities of the body. A *transducer* is any device that takes information in one medium (a change in the concentration of oxygen in the blood, a dimming of the ambient light, a rise in temperature) and translates it into another medium. A photoelectric cell transduces light, in the form of impinging photons, into an electronic signal, in the form of electrons streaming through a wire. A microphone transduces sound waves into signals in the same electronic medium. A bimetallic spring in a thermostat transduces changes in ambient temperature into a bending of the spring (and that, in turn, is typically translated into the transmission of an electronic signal down a wire to turn a heater on or off). The rods and cones in the retina of the eye are the transducers of light into the medium of nerve signals; the eardrum transduces sound waves into vibrations, which eventually get transduced (by the hair cells on the basilar membrane) into the same medium of nerve signals. There are temperature transducers distributed throughout the body, and motion transducers (in the inner ear), and a host of other transducers of other information. An *effector* is any device that can be directed, by some signal in some medium, to make something happen in another "medium" (to bend an arm, close a pore, secrete a fluid, make a noise).

In a computer, there is a nice neat boundary between the "outside" world and the information channels. The input devices, such as the keys on the keyboard, the mouse, the microphone, the television camera, all transduce information into a common medium—the electronic medium in which "bits" are transmitted, stored, transformed. A computer can have internal transducers too, such as a temperature transducer that "informs" the computer that it is overheating, or a transducer that warns it of irregularities in its power supply, but these count as *input* devices, since they extract information from the (internal) environment and put it in the common medium of information processing.

It would be theoretically clean if we could insulate information channels from "outside" events in a body's nervous system, so that all the important interactions happened at identifiable transducers and effectors. The division of labor this would permit is often very illuminating. Consider a ship with a steering wheel located at some great distance from the rudder it controls. You can connect the wheel to the rudder with ropes, or with gears and bicycle chains, wires and pulleys, or with a hydraulic system of high-pressure hoses filled with oil (or water or whiskey!). In one way or another, these systems transmit to the rudder the energy that the helmsman supplies when turning the wheel. *Or* you can connect the wheel to the rudder with nothing but a few thin wires, through which electronic signals pass. You don't have to transduce the energy, just the information *about* how the helmsman wants the rudder to turn. You can transduce this information from the steering wheel into a signal at one end and put the energy in locally, at the other end, with an effector—a motor of some kind. (You can also add "feedback" messages, which are transduced at the motor-rudder end and sent up to control the resistance-to-turning of the wheel, so that the helmsman can sense the pressure of the water on the rudder as it turns. This feedback is standard, these days, in power steering in automobiles, but was dangerously missing in the early days of power steering.)

If you opt for this sort of system—a pure signaling system that transmits information and almost no energy—then it really makes no difference at all whether the signals are electrons passing through a wire or photons passing through a glass fiber or radio waves passing through empty space. In all these cases, what matters is that the information not be lost or distorted because of the time lags between the turning of the wheel and the turning of the rudder. This is also a key requirement in the energy-transmitting systems—the systems using mechanical linkages, such as chains or wires or hoses. That's why elastic bands are not as good as unstretchable cables, even though the information eventually gets there, and why incompressible oil is better than air in a hydraulic system.*

In modern machines, it is often possible in this way to isolate the control system from the system that is controlled, so that control systems can be readily interchanged with no loss of function. The familiar remote controllers of electronic appliances are obvious examples of this, and so are electronic ignition systems (replacing the old mechanical linkages) and other computer-chip-based devices in automobiles. And up to a point, the same freedom from particular media is a feature of animal nervous systems, whose parts can be quite clearly segregated into the peripheral transducers and effectors and the intermediary transmission pathways. One way of going deaf, for instance, is to lose your auditory nerve to cancer. The

....
*The example of the steering gear has an important historical pedigree. The term "cybernetics" was coined by Norbert Wiener from the Greek word for "helmsman" or "steerer." The word "governor" comes from the same source. These ideas about how control is accomplished by the transmission and processing of information were first clearly formulated by Wiener in *Cybernetics; or, Control and Communication in the Animal and the Machine* (1948).

sound-sensitive parts of the ear are still intact, but the transmission of the results of their work to the rest of the brain has been disrupted. This destroyed avenue can now be replaced by a prosthetic link, a tiny cable made of a different material (wire, just as in a standard computer), and since the interfaces at both ends of the cable can be matched to the requirements of the existing healthy materials, the signals can get through. Hearing is restored. It doesn't matter at all what the medium of transmission is, just as long as the information gets through without loss or distortion.

This important theoretical idea sometimes leads to serious confusions, however. The most seductive confusion could be called the Myth of Double Transduction: first, the nervous system transduces light, sound, temperature, and so forth into neural signals (trains of impulses in nerve fibers) and second, in some special central place, it transduces these trains of impulses into some *other* medium, the medium of consciousness! That's what Descartes thought, and he suggested that the pineal gland, right in the center of the brain, was the place where this second transduction took place—into the mysterious, nonphysical medium of the mind. Today almost no one working on the mind thinks there is any such nonphysical medium. Strangely enough, though, the idea of a second transduction into some special *physical* or *material* medium, in some yet-to-be-identified place in the brain, continues to beguile unwary theorists. It is as if they saw—or thought they saw—that since peripheral activity in the nervous system was mere sensitivity, there had to be some more central place where the sentience was created. After all, a live eyeball, disconnected from the rest of the brain, cannot *see*, has no *conscious visual experience*, so that must happen later, when the mysterious *x* is added to mere sensitivity to yield sentience.

The reasons for the persistent attractiveness of this idea are not hard to find. One is tempted to think that mere nerve impulses couldn't be the stuff of consciousness—that they need translation, somehow, into something else. Otherwise, the nervous system would be like a telephone system without anybody home to answer the phone, or a television network without any viewers—or a ship without a helmsman. It seems as if there has to be some central Agent or Boss or Audience, to take in (to transduce) all the information and *appreciate* it, and then "steer the ship."

The idea that the network *itself*—by virtue of its intricate structure, and hence powers of transformation, and hence capacity for controlling the body—could assume the role of the inner Boss and thus harbor consciousness, seems preposterous. Initially. But some version of this claim is the materialist's best hope. Here is where the very complications that ruin the story of the nervous system as a pure information-processing system can be brought in to help our imaginations, by distributing a portion of the huge task of "appreciation" back into the body.

"MY BODY HAS A MIND OF ITS OWN!"
....

> Nature appears to have built the apparatus of rationality not just on top of the apparatus of biological regulation, but also *from* it and *with* it.
> Antonio Damasio, *Descartes' Error: Emotion, Reason, and the Human Brain*

The medium of information transfer in the nervous system is electrochemical pulses traveling through the long branches of nerve cells—not like electrons traveling through a wire at the speed of light, but in a much-slower-traveling chain reaction. A nerve fiber is a sort of elongated battery, in which chemical differences on the inside and outside of the nerve cell's wall induce electric activities that then propagate along the wall at varying speeds—much faster than molecule packets could be shipped through fluid, but much, much slower than the speed of light. Where nerve cells come in contact with each other, at junctures called synapses, a microeffector/microtransducer interaction takes place: the electrical pulse triggers the release of neurotransmitter molecules, which cross the gap by old-fashioned diffusion (the gap is very narrow) and are then transduced into further electrical pulses. A step backward, one might think, into the ancient world of molecular lock-and-key. Especially when it turns out that in addition to the neurotransmitter molecules (such as glutamate), which seem to be more or less neutral all-purpose synapse crossers, there are a variety of neuromodulator molecules, which, when *they* find the "locks" in the neighboring nerve cells, produce all sorts of changes of their own. Would it be right to say that the nerve cells *transduce* the presence of these neuromodulator molecules, in the same way that other transducers "notice" the presence of antigens, or oxygen, or heat? If so, then there are transducers at virtually every joint in the nervous system, adding input to the stream of information already being carried along by the electrical pulses. And there are also effectors everywhere, secreting neuromodulators and neurotransmitters into the "outside" world of the rest of the body, where they diffuse to produce many different effects. The crisp boundary between the information-processing system and the rest of the world—the rest of the body—breaks down.

It has always been clear that wherever you have transducers and effectors, an information system's "media-neutrality," or multiple realizability, disappears. In order to detect light, for instance, you need something photosensitive—something that will respond swiftly and reliably to photons, amplifying their subatomic arrival into larger-scale events that can trigger still further events. (Rhodopsin is one such photosensitive substance, and this protein has been the material of choice in all natural eyes, from ants to fish to eagles to people. Artificial eyes might use some other photosensitive element, but not just anything will do.) In order to identify and disable an antigen, you need an antibody that has the right shape, since the identification is by the lock-and-key method. This limits the choice of antibody building materials to molecules that can fold up into these shapes, and this severely restricts the molecules' chemical composition—though not completely (as the example of lysozyme varieties shows). In theory, every information-processing system is tied at both ends, you might say, to transducers and effectors whose physical composition is dictated by the jobs they have to do; in between, everything can be accomplished by media-neutral processes.

The control systems for ships, automobiles, oil refineries, and other complex human artifacts are media-neutral, as long as the media used can do the job in the available time. The neural control systems for animals, however, are not really media-neutral—not because the control systems have to be made of particular materials in order to generate that special aura or buzz or whatever, but because they evolved as the control systems of organisms that already were lavishly equipped with highly distributed control systems, and the new systems had to be built on top of, and in deep collaboration with, these earlier systems, creating an astronomically high number of points of transduction. We can occasionally ignore these ubiquitous interpenetrations of different media—as, for instance, when we replace a single nerve highway, like the auditory nerve, with a prosthetic substitute—but only in a fantastic thought experiment could we ignore these interpenetrations *in general*.

For example: The molecular keys needed to unlock the locks that control every transaction between nerve cells are

glutamate molecules, dopamine molecules, and norepineph-
rine molecules (among others); but "in principle" all the
locks could be changed—that is, replaced with a chemically
different system. After all, the function of the chemical
depends on its fit with the lock, and hence on the subsequent effects triggered by the arrival of this turn-on message,
and not on anything else. But the distribution of responsibility throughout the body makes this changing of the locks
practically impossible. Too much of the information processing—and hence information storage—is already embedded
in these particular materials. And that's another good reason
why, when you make a mind, the materials matter. So there
are two good reasons for this: speed, and the ubiquity of
transducers and effectors throughout the nervous system. I
don't think there are any other good reasons.

These considerations lend support to the intuitively
appealing claim often advanced by critics of functionalism:
that it really does matter what you make a mind out of. You
couldn't make a *sentient* mind out of silicon chips, or wire
and glass, or beer cans tied together with string. Are these
reasons for abandoning functionalism? Not at all. In fact, they
depend on the basic insight of functionalism for their force.

The *only* reason minds depend on the chemical composition of their mechanisms or media is that in order to do the
things these mechanisms must do, they have to be made, as
a matter of biohistorical fact, from substances compatible
with the preexisting bodies they control. Functionalism is
opposed to vitalism and other forms of mysticism about the
"intrinsic properties" of various substances. There is no
more anger or fear in adrenaline than there is silliness in a
bottle of whiskey. These substances, per se, are as irrelevant
to the mental as gasoline or carbon dioxide. It is only when
their abilities to function as components of larger functional
systems depend on their internal composition that their so-
called "intrinsic nature" matters.

The fact that your nervous system, unlike the control system of a modern ship, is not an insulated, media-neutral control system—the fact that it "effects" and "transduces" at almost every juncture—forces us to think about the functions of their parts in a more complicated (and realistic) way. This recognition makes life slightly more difficult for functionalist philosophers of mind. A thousand philosophical thought experiments (including my own story, "Where am I?" [1978]) have exploited the intuition that *I* am not my body but my body's . . . owner. In a heart transplant operation, you want to be the recipient, not the donor, but in a brain transplant operation, you want to be the donor—you go with the brain, not the body. In principle (as many philosophers have argued), *I* might even trade in my current brain for another, by replacing the medium while preserving only the message. I could travel by teleportation, for instance, as long as the information was perfectly preserved. In principle, yes—but only because one would be transmitting information about the whole body, not just the nervous system. One cannot tear me apart from my body leaving a nice clean edge, as philosophers have often supposed. My body contains as much of *me*, the values and talents and memories and dispositions that make me who I am, as my nervous system does.

The legacy of Descartes's notorious dualism of mind and body extends far beyond academia into everyday thinking: "These athletes are prepared both mentally and physically," and "There's nothing wrong with your body—it's all in your mind." Even among those of us who have battled Descartes's vision, there has been a powerful tendency to treat the mind (that is to say, the brain) as the body's boss, the pilot of the ship. Falling in with this standard way of thinking, we ignore an important alternative: viewing the brain (and hence the mind) as one organ among many, a relatively recent usurper of control, whose functions cannot properly be understood until we see it not as the boss but as just one more somewhat fractious servant, working to further the interests of the body that shelters and fuels it and gives its activities meaning.

This historical or evolutionary perspective reminds me of the change that has come over Oxford in the thirty years since I was a student there. It used to be that the dons were in charge, and the bursars and other bureaucrats, right up to the vice chancellor, acted under their guidance and at their behest. Nowadays the dons, like their counterparts on American university faculties, are more clearly in the role of employees hired by a central administration. But from where, finally, does the University get its meaning? In evolutionary history, a similar change has crept over the administration of our bodies. But our bodies, like the Oxford dons, still have some power of decision—or, at any rate, some power to rebel when the central administration acts in ways that run counter to the sentiments of "the body politic."

It is harder to think functionalistically about the mind once we abandon the crisp identification of the mind with the brain and let it spread to other parts of the body, but the compensations are enormous. The fact that our control systems, unlike those of ships and other artifacts, are so noninsulated permits our bodies themselves (as distinct from the nervous systems they contain) to harbor much of the wisdom that "we" exploit in the course of daily decision making. Friedrich Nietzsche saw all this long ago, and put the case with characteristic brio, in *Thus Spake Zarathustra* (in the section aptly entitled "On the Despisers of the Body"):

"Body am I, and soul"—thus speaks the child. And why should one not speak like children? But the awakened and knowing say: body am I entirely, and nothing else; and soul is only a word for something about the body.

The body is a great reason, a plurality with one sense, a war and a peace, a herd and a shepherd. An instrument of your body is also your little reason, my brother, which you call "spirit"—a little instrument and toy of your great reason. . . . Behind your thoughts and feelings, my brother, there stands a mighty ruler, an unknown sage— whose name is self. In your body he dwells; he is your body. There is more reason in your body than in your best wisdom. (Kaufmann translation, 1954, p. 146)

Evolution embodies information in every part of every organism. A whale's baleen embodies information about the food it eats, and the liquid medium in which it finds its food. A bird's wing embodies information about the medium in which it does its work. A chameleon's skin, more dramatically, carries information about its current environment. An animal's viscera and hormonal systems embody a great deal of information about the world in which its ancestors have lived. This information doesn't have to be copied into the brain at all. It doesn't have to be "represented" in "data structures" in the nervous system. It can be exploited by the nervous system, however, which is designed to rely on, or exploit, the information in the hormonal systems just as it is designed to rely on, or exploit, the information embodied in the limbs and eyes. So there is wisdom, particularly about preferences, embodied in the rest of the body. By using the old bodily systems as a sort of sounding board, or reactive audience, or critic, the central nervous system can be guided—sometimes nudged, sometimes slammed—into wise policies. Put it to the vote of the body, in effect. To be fair to poor old Descartes, we should note that even he saw—at least dimly—the importance of this union of body and mind:

By means of these feelings of pain, hunger, thirst, and so on, nature also teaches that I am present to my body not merely in the way a seaman is present to his ship, but that I am tightly joined and, so to speak, mingled together with it, so much so that I make up one single thing with it. (Meditation Six)

When all goes well, harmony reigns and the various sources of wisdom in the body cooperate for the benefit of the whole, but we are all too familiar with the conflicts that can provoke the curious outburst "My body has a mind of its own!" Sometimes, apparently, it is tempting to lump together some of this embodied information into a *separate* mind. Why? Because it is organized in such a way that it can sometimes make somewhat independent discriminations, consult preferences, make decisions, enact policies that are in competition with *your* mind. At such times, the Cartesian perspective of a puppeteer self trying desperately to control an unruly body-puppet is very powerful. Your body can vigorously betray the secrets *you* are desperately trying to keep—by blushing and trembling or sweating, to mention only the most obvious cases. It can "decide" that in spite of *your* well-laid plans, right now would be a good time for sex, not intellectual discussion, and then take embarrassing steps in preparation for a coup d'état. On another occasion, to your even greater chagrin and frustration, it can turn a deaf ear on your own efforts to enlist it for a sexual campaign, forcing you to raise the volume, twirl the dials, try all manner of preposterous cajolings to *persuade* it.

But why, if our bodies already had minds of their own, did they ever go about acquiring additional minds—*our* minds? Isn't one mind per body enough? Not always. As we have seen, the old body-based minds have done a robust job of keeping life and limb together over billions of years, but they are relatively slow and relatively crude in their discriminatory powers. Their intentionality is short-range and easily tricked. For more sophisticated engagements with the world, a swifter, farther-seeing mind is called for, one that can produce more and better future.

....

CHAPTER 4

HOW INTENTIONALITY
CAME INTO FOCUS

THE TOWER OF GENERATE-AND-TEST*

....

In order to see farther ahead in time, it helps to see farther into space. What began as internal and peripheral monitoring systems slowly evolved into systems that were capable of not just proximal (neighboring) but distal (distant) discrimination. This is where perception comes into its own. The sense of smell, or olfaction, relies on the wafting from afar of harbinger keys to local locks. The trajectories of these harbingers are relatively slow, variable, and uncertain, because of random dispersal and evaporation; thus information about the source they emanate from is limited. Hearing depends on sound waves striking the system's transducers, and because the paths of sound waves are swifter and more regular, perception can come closer to approximating "action at a distance." But sound waves can deflect and bounce in ways that obscure their source. Vision depends on

....

*This section is drawn, with revisions, from *Darwin's Dangerous Idea*.

the much swifter arrival of photons bounced off the things in the world, on definitively straight-line trajectories, so that with a suitably shaped pinhole (and optional lens) arrangement, an organism can obtain instantaneous high-fidelity information about events and surfaces far away. How did this transition from internal to proximal to distal intentionality take place? Evolution created armies of specialized internal agents to receive the information available at the peripheries of the body. There is just as much information encoded in the light that falls on a pine tree as there is in the light that falls on a squirrel, but the squirrel is equipped with millions of information-seeking microagents, specifically designed to take in, and even to seek out and interpret this information.

Animals are not just herbivores or carnivores. They are, in the nice coinage of the psychologist George Miller, *informavores*. And they get their epistemic hunger from the combination, in exquisite organization, of the specific epistemic hungers of millions of microagents, organized into dozens or hundreds or thousands of subsystems. Each of these tiny agents can be conceived of as an utterly minimal intentional system, whose life project is to ask a single question, over and over and over—"Is my message coming in NOW?" "Is my message coming in NOW?"—and springing into limited but appropriate action whenever the answer is YES. Without the epistemic hunger, there is no perception, no uptake. Philosophers have often attempted to analyze perception into the Given and what is then done with the Given by the mind. The Given is, of course, Taken, but the taking of the Given is not something done by one Master Taker located in some central headquarters of the animal's brain. The task of taking is distributed among all the individually organized takers. The takers are not just the peripheral transducers— the rods and cones on the retina of the eye, the specialized cells in the epithelium of the nose—but also all the internal functionaries fed by them, cells and groups of cells connected in networks throughout the brain. They are fed not patterns of light or pressure (the pressure of sound waves and of touch) but patterns of neuronal impulses; but aside from the change of diet, they are playing similar roles. How do all these agents get organized into larger systems capable of sustaining ever more sophisticated sorts of intentionality? By a process of evolution by natural selection, of course, but not just one process.

I want to propose a framework in which we can place the various design options for brains, to see where their power comes from. It is an outrageously oversimplified structure, but idealization is the price one should often be willing to pay for synoptic insight. I call it the Tower of Generate-and-Test. As each new floor of the Tower gets constructed, it empowers the organisms at that level to find better and better moves, and find them more efficiently.

The increasing power of organisms to produce future can be represented, then, in a series of steps. These steps almost certainly don't represent clearly defined transitional periods in evolutionary history—no doubt such steps were taken in overlapping and nonuniform ways by different lineages—but the various floors of the Tower of Generate-and-Test mark important advances in cognitive power, and once we see in outline a few of the highlights of each stage, the rest of the evolutionary steps will make more sense.

In the beginning, there was Darwinian evolution of species by natural selection. A variety of candidate organisms were blindly generated, by more or less arbitrary processes of recombination and mutation of genes. These organisms were field-tested, and only the best designs survived. This is the ground floor of the tower. Let us call its inhabitants *Darwinian creatures*.

This process went through many millions of cycles, producing many wonderful designs, both plant and animal.

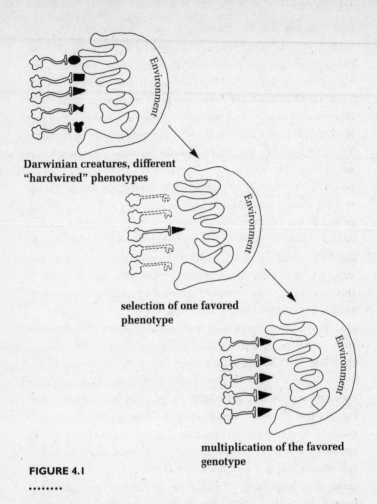

Darwinian creatures, different "hardwired" phenotypes

selection of one favored phenotype

multiplication of the favored genotype

FIGURE 4.1

· · · · · · · · ·

Eventually, among its novel creations were some designs with the property of *phenotypic plasticity*: that is, the individual candidate organisms were not wholly designed at birth; there were elements of their design that could be *adjusted by events that occurred during the field tests*. Some of these candidates, we may suppose, were no better off than their cousins, the hardwired Darwinian creatures, since they had no way of favoring (selecting for an encore) the behavioral options they were equipped to "try out." But others, we may suppose, were fortunate enough to have wired-in "reinforcers" that happened to favor Smart Moves—that is, actions that were better for the candidates than the available alternative actions. These individuals thus confronted the environment by generating a variety of actions, which they tried out, one by one, until they found one that worked. They detected that it worked only by getting a positive or negative signal from the environment, which adjusted the probability of that action's being reproduced on another occasion. Any creatures wired up wrong—with positive and negative reinforcement reversed—would be doomed, of course. Only those fortunate enough to be born with appropriate reinforcers would have an advantage. We may call this subset of Darwinian creatures *Skinnerian creatures*, since, as the behaviorist psychologist B. F. Skinner was fond of pointing out, such "operant conditioning" is not just analogous to Darwinian natural selection; it is an extension of it: "Where inherited behavior leaves off, the inherited modifiability of the process of conditioning takes over." (1953, p. 83)

The cognitive revolution that emerged in the 1970s ousted behaviorism from its dominant position in psychology, and ever since there has been a tendency to underestimate the power of Skinnerian conditioning (or its variations) to shape the behavioral competence of organisms into highly adaptive and discerning structures. The flourishing work on neural networks and "connectionism" in the 1990s, however, has demonstrated anew the often surprising virtuosity of simple networks that begin life more or less randomly wired and then have their connections adjusted by a simple sort of "experience"—the history of reinforcement they encounter.

The fundamental idea of letting the environment play a blind but selective role in shaping the mind (or brain or control system) has a pedigree even older than Darwin. The intellectual ancestors of today's connectionists and yester-

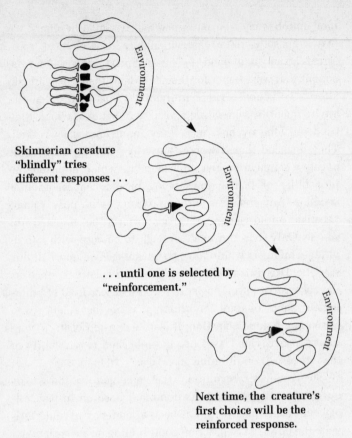

Skinnerian creature "blindly" tries different responses . . .

. . . until one is selected by "reinforcement."

Next time, the creature's first choice will be the reinforced response.

FIGURE 4.2
....

day's behaviorists were the associationists: such philosophers as David Hume, who tried in the eighteenth century to imagine how mind parts (he called them impressions and ideas) could become self-organizing without benefit of some all-too-knowing director of the organization. As a student once memorably said to me, "Hume wanted to get the ideas to think for themselves." Hume had wonderful hunches about how impressions and ideas might link themselves together by a process rather like chemical bonding, and then create beaten paths of habit in the mind, but these hunches were too vague to be tested. Hume's associationism was, however, a direct inspiration for Pavlov's famous experiments in the conditioning of animal behavior, which led in turn to the somewhat different conditioning theories of E. L. Thorndike, Skinner, and the other behaviorists in psychology. Some of these researchers—Donald Hebb, in particular—attempted to link their behaviorism more closely to what was then known about the brain. In 1949, Hebb proposed models of simple conditioning mechanisms that could adjust the connections between nerve cells. These mechanisms—now called Hebbian learning rules—and their descendants are the engines of change in connectionism, the latest manifestation of this tradition.

Associationism, behaviorism, connectionism—in historical and alphabetical order we can trace the evolution of models of one simple kind of learning, which might well be called *ABC learning.* There is no doubt that most animals are capable of ABC learning; that is, they can come to modify (or redesign) their behavior in appropriate directions as a result of a long, steady process of training or shaping by the environment. There are now good models, in varying degrees of realism and detail, of how such a process of conditioning or training can be nonmiraculously accomplished in a network of nerve cells.

For many life-saving purposes (pattern recognition, discrimination, and generalization, and the dynamical control of locomotion, for instance), ABC networks are quite wonderful—efficient, compact, robust in performance, fault-tolerant, and relatively easy to redesign on the fly. Such networks, moreover, vividly emphasize Skinner's point that it makes little difference where we draw the line between the pruning and shaping by natural selection which is genetically transmitted to offspring (the wiring you are born with), and the pruning and shaping that later takes place in the individual (the rewiring you end up with, as a result of experience or training). Nature and nurture blend seamlessly together.

There are, however, some cognitive tricks that such ABC networks have not yet been trained to perform, and—a more telling criticism—there are some cognitive tricks that are quite clearly not the result of training at all. Some animals seem to be capable of "one-shot learning"; they can figure some things out without having to endure the arduous process of trial-and-error in the harsh world that is the hallmark of all ABC learning.

Skinnerian conditioning is a good thing as long as you are not killed by one of your early errors. A better system involves *preselection* among all the possible behaviors or actions, so that the truly stupid moves are weeded out before they're hazarded in "real life." We human beings are creatures capable of this particular refinement, but we are not alone. We may call the beneficiaries of this third floor in the Tower *Popperian creatures*, since, as the philosopher Sir Karl Popper once elegantly put it, this design enhancement "permits our hypotheses to die in our stead." Unlike the merely Skinnerian creatures, many of whom survive only because they make lucky first moves, Popperian creatures survive because they're smart enough to make better-than-chance first moves. Of course they're just lucky to be smart, but that's better than being just lucky.

How is this preselection in Popperian agents to be done? There must be a filter, and any such filter must amount to a sort of *inner environment,* in which tryouts can be safely executed—an inner something-or-other structured in such a way that the surrogate actions it favors are more often than not the very actions the real world would also bless, if they were actually performed. In short, the inner environment, whatever it is, must contain lots of *information* about the outer environment and its regularities. Nothing else (except magic) could provide preselection worth having. (One could always flip a coin or consult an oracle, but this is no improvement over blind trial and error—unless the coin or oracle is systematically biased by someone or something that has true information about the world.)

The beauty of Popper's idea is exemplified in the recent development of realistic flight simulators used for training airplane pilots. In a simulated world, pilots can learn which moves to execute in which crises without ever risking their lives (or expensive airplanes). As examples of the Popperian trick, however, flight simulators are in one regard misleading: they reproduce the real world too literally. We must be very careful not to think of the inner environment of a Popperian creature as simply a replica of the outer world, with all the physical contingencies of that world reproduced. In such a miraculous toy world, the little hot stove in your head would be hot enough to actually burn the little finger in your head that you placed on it! Nothing of the sort needs to be supposed. The *information* about the effect of putting a

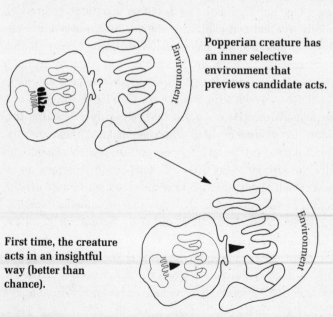

Popperian creature has an inner selective environment that previews candidate acts.

First time, the creature acts in an insightful way (better than chance).

FIGURE 4.3

finger on the stove has to be in there, and it has to be in there in a form that can produce its premonitory effect when called upon in an internal trial, but this effect can be achieved without constructing a replica world. After all, it would be equally Popperian to educate pilots just by having them read a book that explained to them all the contingencies they might encounter when they eventually climbed into the cockpit. It might not be as powerful a method of learning, but it would be hugely better than trial-and-error in the sky! The common element in Popperian creatures is that one way or another (either by inheritance or by acquisition) information is installed in them—accurate information about the world that they (probably) will encounter—and this information is in such a form that it can achieve the preselective effects that are its raison d'être.

One of the ways Popperian creatures achieve useful filtering is by putting candidate behavioral options before the bodily tribunal and exploiting the wisdom, however out-of-date or shortsighted, accumulated in those tissues. If the body rebels—for example, in such typical reactions as nausea, vertigo, or fear and trembling—this is a semireliable sign (better than a coin flip) that the contemplated act might not be a good idea. Here we see that rather than rewiring the brain to eliminate these choices, making them strictly unthinkable, evolution may simply arrange to respond to any thinking of them with a negative rush so strong as to make them highly unlikely to win the competition for execution. The information in the body that grounds the reaction may have been placed there either by genetic recipe or by recent individual experience. When a human infant first learns to crawl, it has an innate aversion to venturing out onto a pane of supportive glass, through which it can see a "visual cliff." Even though its mother beckons it from a few feet away, cajoling and encouraging, the infant hangs back fearfully, despite never having suffered a fall in its life. The experience of its ancestors is making it err on the side of safety. When a rat has eaten a new kind of food and has then been injected with a drug that causes it to vomit, it will subsequently show a strong aversion to food that looks and smells like the food it ate just before vomiting. Here the information leading it to err on the side of safety was obtained from its own experience. Neither filter is perfect—after all, the pane of glass is actually safe, and the rat's new food is actually nontoxic—but better safe than sorry.

Clever experiments by psychologists and ethologists suggest other ways in which animals can try actions out "in their heads" and thereby reap a Popperian benefit. In the 1930s and 1940s, behaviorists demonstrated to themselves time and again that their experimental animals were capable of "latent learning" about the world—learning that was not specifically rewarded by any detectable reinforcement. (Their exercise in self-refutation is itself a prime example of another Popperian theme: that science makes progress only when it poses refutable hypotheses.) If left to explore a maze in which no food or other reward was present, rats would simply learn their way around in the normal course of things; then, if something they valued was introduced into the maze, the rats that had learned their way around on earlier forays were much better at finding it (not surprisingly) than the rats in the control group, which were seeing the maze for the first time. This may seem a paltry discovery. Wasn't it always obvious that rats were smart enough to learn their way around? Yes and no. It may have *seemed* obvious, but this is just the sort of testing—testing against the background of the null hypothesis—that must be conducted if we are going to be sure just how intelligent, how mindful, various species are. As we shall see, other experiments with animals demonstrate surprisingly stupid streaks—almost unbelievable gaps in the animals' knowledge of their own environments.

The behaviorists tried valiantly to accommodate latent learning into their ABC models. One of their most telling stopgaps was to postulate a "curiosity drive," which was satisfied (or "reduced," as they said) by exploration. There was reinforcement going on after all in those nonreinforcing environments. Every environment, marvelous to say, is full of reinforcing stimuli simply by being an environment in which there is something to learn. As an attempt to save orthodox behaviorism, this move was manifestly vacuous, but that does not make it a hopeless idea in other contexts; it acknowledges the fact that curiosity—epistemic hunger— must drive any powerful learning system.

We human beings are conditionable by ABC training, so we are Skinnerian creatures, but we are not *just* Skinnerian creatures. We also enjoy the benefits of much genetically inherited hardwiring, so we are Darwinian creatures as well. But we are more than that. We are Popperian creatures. Which other animals are Popperian creatures, and which are merely Skinnerian? Pigeons were Skinner's favorite experimental animals, and he and his followers developed the technology of operant conditioning to a very sophisticated level, getting pigeons to exhibit remarkably bizarre and sophisticated learned behaviors. Notoriously, the Skinnerians never succeeded in proving that pigeons were *not* Popperian creatures; and research on a host of different species, from octopuses to fish to mammals, strongly suggests that if there are any purely Skinnerian creatures, capable only of blind trial-and-error learning, they are to be found among the simple invertebrates. The huge sea slug (or sea hare) *Aplysia californica* has more or less replaced the pigeon as the focus of attention among those who study the mechanisms of simple conditioning.

We do not differ from all other species in being Popperian creatures then. Far from it; mammals and birds, reptiles, amphibians, fish, and even many invertebrates exhibit the capacity to use general information they obtain from their environments to presort their behavioral options before striking out. How does the new information about the outer environment get incorporated into their brains? By perception, obviously. The environment contains an embarrassment of riches, much more information than even a cognitive angel could use. Perceptual mechanisms designed to ignore most of the flux of stimuli concentrate on the most useful, most reliable information. And how does the information gathered manage to exert its selective effect when the options are "considered," helping the animal design ever more effective interactions with its world? There are no doubt a variety of different mechanisms and methods, but among them are those that use the body as a sounding board.

THE SEARCH FOR SENTIENCE: A PROGRESS REPORT
········

We have been gradually adding elements to our recipe for a mind. Do we have the ingredients for sentience yet? Certainly the normal behavior of many of the animals we have been describing passes our intuitive tests for sentience with flying colors. Watching a puppy or a baby tremble with fear at the edge of an apparent precipice, or a rat grimacing in apparent disgust at the odor of supposedly toxic food, we have difficulty even entertaining the hypothesis that we are *not* witnessing a sentient being. But we have also uncovered substantial grounds for caution: we have seen some ways in which surprisingly mindlike behavior can be produced by relatively simple, mechanical, apparently unmindlike control systems. The potency of our instinctual responses to sheer speed and lifelikeness of motion, for instance, should alert us to the genuine—not merely philosophical—possibility that we can be fooled into attributing more subtlety, more understanding, to an entity than the circumstances warrant. Recognizing that observable behavior can enchant us, we can appreciate the need to ask further questions—about what lies behind that behavior.

Consider pain. In 1986, the British government amended its laws protecting animals in experiments, adding the octopus to the privileged circle of animals that may not be operated upon without anesthesia. An octopus is a mollusk, physiologically more like an oyster than a trout (let alone a mammal), but the behavior of the octopus and the other cephalopods (squid, cuttlefish) is so strikingly intelligent and—apparently—sentient that the scientific authorities decided to let behavioral similarity override internal difference: cephalopods (but not other mollusks) are officially presumed to be capable of feeling pain—just in case they are. Rhesus monkeys, in contrast, are physiologically and evolutionarily very close to us, so we tend to assume that they are capable of suffering the way we do, but they exhibit astonishingly different behavior on occasion. The primatologist Marc Hauser has told me in conversation that during mating season the male monkeys fight ferociously, and it is not uncommon to see one male pin another down and then bite and rip out one of its testicles. The injured male does not shriek or make a facial expression but simply licks the wound and walks away. A day or two later, the wounded animal may be observed mating! It is hard to believe that this animal was experiencing anything like the agonies of a human being similarly afflicted—the mind reels to think of it—in spite of our biological kinship. So we can no longer hope that the physiological and behaviorial evidence will happily converge to give us unequivocal answers, since we already know cases in which these two sorts of compelling if inconclusive evidence pull in opposite directions. How then can we think about this issue?

A key function of pain is negative reinforcement—the "punishment" that diminishes the likelihood of a repeat performance—and any Skinnerian creature can be trained by negative reinforcement of one sort or another. Is all such negative reinforcement pain? *Experienced* pain? Could there be unconscious or unexperienced *pain*? There are simple mechanisms of negative reinforcement that provide the behavior-shaping or pruning power of pain with apparently no further mindlike effects, so it would be a mistake to invoke sentience wherever we find Skinnerian conditioning. Another function of pain is to disrupt normal patterns of bodily activity that might exacerbate an injury—pain causes an animal to favor an injured limb until it can mend, for instance—and this is normally accomplished by a flood of neurochemicals in a self-sustaining loop of interaction with the nervous system. Does the presence of those substances then guarantee the occurrence of pain? No, for in themselves they are just keys floating around in search of their locks; if the cycle of interaction is interrupted, there is no reason at all to suppose that pain persists. Are these particular substances even necessary for pain? Might there be creatures with a different system of locks and keys? The answer may depend more on historical processes of evolution on this planet than on any intrinsic properties of the substances. The example of the octopus shows that we should look to see what variations in chemical implementation are to be found, with what differences in function, but without expecting these facts *in themselves* to settle our question about sentience.

What then about the other features of this cycle of interaction? How rudimentary might a pain system be and still count as sentience? What would be relevant and why? Consider, for instance, a toad with a broken leg. Is this a sentient being experiencing pain? It is a living being whose normal life has been disrupted by damage to one of its parts, preventing it from engaging in the behaviors that are its way of earning a living. It is moreover in a state with powerful negative-reinforcement potential—it can readily be conditioned to avoid such states of its nervous system. This state is maintained by a cycle of interaction that somewhat disrupts its normal dispositions to leap—though in an emergency it will leap anyway. It is tempting to see all this as amounting to pain. But it is also tempting to endow the toad with a soliloquy, in which it dreads the prospect of such an emergency, yearns for relief, deplores its relative vulnerability, bitterly regrets the foolish actions that led it to this crisis, and so forth, and these further accompaniments are not in any way licensed by anything we know about toads. On the contrary, the more we learn about toads, the more confident we are becoming that their nervous systems are designed to carry them through life without any such expensive reflective capacities.

So what? What does *sentience* have to do with such fancy intellectual talents? A good question, but that means we must try to answer it, and not just use it as a rhetorical question to deflect inquiry. Here is a circumstance in which how we ask the questions can make a huge difference, for it is possible to bamboozle ourselves into creating a phantom problem at this point. How? By losing track of where we stand in a process of addition and subtraction. At the outset, we are searching for x, the special ingredient that distinguishes mere sensitivity from true sentience, and we work on the project from two directions. Working up from simple cases, adding rudimentary versions of each separate feature, we tend to be unimpressed: though each of these powers is arguably an essential component of sentience, there is surely more to sentience than that—a mere robot could well exhibit *that* without any sentience at all! Working down, from our own richly detailed (and richly appreciated) experience, we recognize that other creatures manifestly lack some of the particularly human features of our experience, so we subtract them as inessential. We don't want to be unfair to our animal cousins. So while we recognize that much of what we think of when we think of the awfulness of pain (and why it matters morally whether someone is in pain) involves imagining just these anthropomorphic accompaniments, we generously decide that they are just accompaniments, not "essential" to the brute phenomenon of sentience (and its morally most significant instance, pain). What we may tend to overlook, as these two ships pass in the night, is the possibility that we are subtracting, on one path, the very thing we are seeking on the other. *If* that's what we're doing, our conviction that we have yet to come across *x*—the "missing link" of sentience—would be a self-induced illusion.

I don't say that we *are* making an error of this sort, but just that we *might well* be doing so. That's enough for the moment, since it shifts the burden of proof. Here, then, is a conservative hypothesis about the problem of sentience: There is no such *extra* phenomenon. "Sentience" comes in every imaginable grade or intensity, from the simplest and most "robotic," to the most exquisitely sensitive, hyper-reactive "human." As we saw in chapter 1, we do indeed have to draw lines across this multistranded continuum of cases, because having moral policies requires it, but the prospect that we will *discover* a threshold—a morally significant "step," in what is otherwise a ramp—is not only extremely unlikely but morally unappealing as well.

Consider the toad once again in this regard. On which side of the line does the toad fall? (If toads are too obvious a case for you one way or the other, choose whatever creature seems to occupy your penumbra of uncertainty. Choose an ant or a jellyfish or a pigeon or a rat.) Now suppose that "science confirms" that there is minimal genuine sentience in the toad—that a toad's "pain" is real, experienced pain, for instance. The toad now qualifies for the special treatment reserved for the sentient. Now suppose instead that the toad turns out not to have *x*, once we have determined what *x* is.

In this case, the toad's status falls to "mere automaton," something that we may interfere with in any imaginable way with no moral compunction whatever. Given what we *already* know about toads, does it seem plausible that there could be some *heretofore unimagined* feature the discovery of which could justify this enormous difference in our attitude? Of course, if we discovered that toads were really tiny human beings trapped in toad bodies, like the prince in the fairy tale, we would immediately have grounds for the utmost solicitude, for we would know that in spite of all behavioral appearances, toads *were* capable of enduring all the tortures and anxieties we consider so important in our own cases. But we already know that a toad is no such thing. We are being asked to imagine that there is some x that is nothing at all like being a human prince trapped in a toad skin, but is nevertheless morally compelling. We also already know, however, that a toad is not a simple wind-up toy but rather an exquisitely complex living thing capable of a staggering variety of self-protective activities in the furtherance of its preordained task of making more generations of toads. Isn't that already enough to warrant some special regard on our part? We are being asked to imagine that there is some x that is nothing at all like this mere sophistication-of-control-structure, but that nevertheless would command our moral appreciation when we discovered it. We are being asked, I suspect, to indulge in something beyond fantasy. But let us continue with our search, to see what comes next, for we are still a long way from human minds.

FROM PHOTOTAXIS TO METAPHYSICS
....

Once we get to Popperian creatures—creatures whose brains have the potential to be endowed, in inner environments, with preselective prowess—what happens next? Many different things, no doubt, but we will concentrate on one particular innovation whose powers we can clearly see. Among the successors to mere Popperian creatures are those whose inner environments are informed by the *designed* portions of the outer environment. One of Darwin's fundamental insights is that design is expensive but copying designs is cheap; that is, making an all new design is very difficult, but redesigning old designs is relatively easy. Few of us could reinvent the wheel, but we don't have to, since we acquired the wheel design (and a huge variety of others) from the cultures we grew up in. We may call this sub-sub-subset of Darwinian creatures *Gregorian creatures*, since the British psychologist Richard Gregory is to my mind the preeminent theorist of the role of information (or more exactly, what Gregory calls Potential Intelligence) in the creation of Smart Moves (or what Gregory calls Kinetic Intelligence). Gregory observes that a pair of scissors, as a well-designed artifact, is not just a result of intelligence but an endower of intelligence (external potential intelligence), in a very straightforward and intuitive sense: when you give someone a pair of scissors, you enhance their potential to arrive more safely and swiftly at Smart Moves. (1981, pp. 311ff.)

Anthropologists have long recognized that the advent of tool use accompanied a major increase in intelligence. Chimpanzees in the wild go after termites by thrusting crudely prepared fishing sticks deep into the termites' underground homes and swiftly drawing up a stickful of termites, which they then strip off the stick into their mouths. This fact takes on further significance when we learn that not all chimpanzees have hit upon this trick; in some chimpanzee "cultures," termites are an unexploited food source. This reminds us that tool use is a two-way sign of intelligence; not only does it *require* intelligence to recognize and maintain a tool (let alone fabricate one), but a tool *confers* intelligence on those lucky enough to be given one. The better designed the tool (the more information there is embedded in its fabrication), the more potential intelligence it confers on its user. And among the preeminent tools, Gregory reminds us, are what he calls mind tools: words.

Words and other mind tools give a Gregorian creature an inner environment that permits it to construct ever more subtle move generators and move testers. Skinnerian creatures ask themselves, "What do I do next?" and haven't a clue how to answer until they have taken some hard knocks. Popperian creatures make a big advance by asking themselves, "What should I think about next?" before they ask themselves, "What should I do next?" (It should be emphasized that neither Skinnerian nor Popperian creatures actually need to talk to themselves or think these thoughts. They are simply designed to operate *as if* they had asked themselves these questions. Here we see both the power and the risk of the intentional stance: The reason that Popperian creatures are smarter—more successfully devious, say—than Skinnerian creatures is that they are adaptively responsive

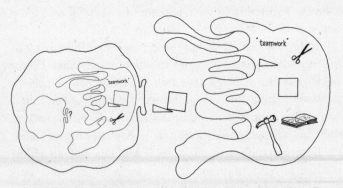

Gregorian creature imports mind tools from the (cultural) environment; these improve both the generators and the testers.

FIGURE 4.4

· · · · · · · ·

to more and better information, in a way that we can vividly if loosely describe from the intentional stance, in terms of these imaginary soliloquies. But it would be a mistake to impute to these creatures all the subtleties that go along with the ability to actually formulate such questions and answers on the human model of explicit self-questioning.) Gregorian creatures take a big step toward a human level of mental adroitness, benefiting from the experience of others by exploiting the wisdom embodied in the mind tools that those others have invented, improved, and transmitted; thereby they learn how to think better about what they should think about next—and so forth, creating a tower of further internal reflections with no fixed or discernible limit. How this step to the Gregorian level might be accomplished can best be seen by once more backing up and looking at the ancestral talents from which these most human mental talents must be constructed.

One of the simplest life-enhancing practices found in many species is *phototaxis*—distinguishing light from dark and heading for the light. Light is easily transduced, and given the way light emanates from a source, its intensity diminishing gradually as you get farther away, quite a simple connection between transducers and effectors can produce reliable phototaxis. In the neuroscientist Valentino Braitenberg's elegant little book *Vehicles*, we get the simplest model—the vehicle in figure 4.5. It has two light transducers, and their variable output signals are fed, crossed, to two effectors (think of the effectors as outboard motors). The more light transduced, the faster the motor runs. The transducer nearer the light source will drive its motor a bit faster than the transducer farther from the light, and this will always turn the vehicle in the direction of the light, till eventually it hits the light source itself or orbits tightly around it.

The world of such a simple being is graded from light to not-so-light to dark, and it traverses the gradient. It knows,

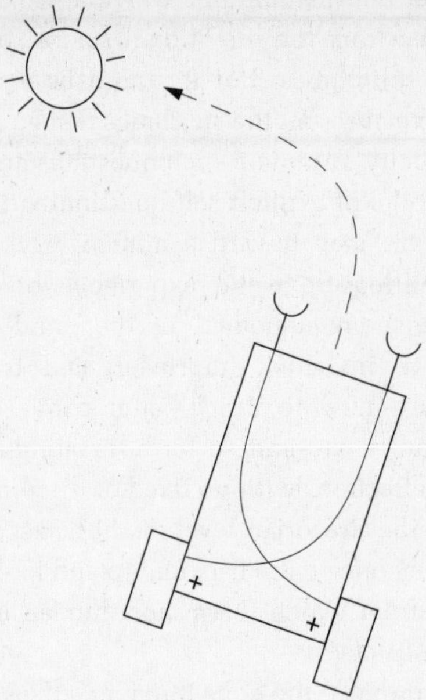

FIGURE 4.5

∙∙∙∙∙∙∙∙

and needs to know, nothing else. Light *recognition* is almost for free—whatever turns on the transducer is light, and the system doesn't care whether it's the very *same* light that has returned or a new light. In a world with two moons, it might make a difference, ecologically, which moon you were tracking; moon recognition or identification could be an additional problem that needed a solution. Mere phototaxis would not be enough in such a world. In our world, a moon is not the sort of object that typically needs reidentifying by a creature; mothers, in contrast, often are.

Mamataxis—homing in on Mother—is a considerably more sophisticated talent. If Mama emitted a bright light, phototaxis might do the job, but not if there were other mothers in the vicinity, all using the same system. If Mama then emitted a particular blue light, different from the light emitted by every other mother, then putting a particular everything-but-blue filter on each of your phototransducers would do the job quite well. Nature often relies on a similar principle, but using a more energy-efficient medium. Mama emits a signature odor, distinguishably different from all other odors (in the immediate vicinity). Mamataxis (mother-reidentification and homing) is then accomplished by odor-transduction, or olfaction. The intensity of odors is a function of the concentration of the molecular keys as they diffuse through the surrounding medium—air or water. A transducer can therefore be an appropriately shaped lock, and can follow the gradient of concentration by using an arrangement just like that in Braitenberg's vehicle. Such olfactory signatures are ancient, and potent. They have been overlaid, in our species, by thousands of other mechanisms, but their position in the foundation is still discernible. In spite of all our sophistication, odors *move* us without our knowing why or how, as Marcel Proust famously noted.*

Technology honors the same design principle in yet another medium: the EPIRB (Emergency Position Indicating Radio Beacon), a self-contained, battery-powered radio transmitter that repeats over and over again a particular signature at a particular frequency. You can buy one in a marine hardware store and take it with you on your sailboat. Then if you ever get in distress, you turn it on. Immediately

....
*Odors are not used only for identification signals. They often play powerful roles in attracting a mate or even suppressing the sexual activity or maturation of one's rivals. Signals from the olfactory bulb bypass the thalamus on their way to the rest of the brain, so in contrast to the signals arising in vision, hearing, and even touch, olfactory commands go directly to the old control centers, eliminating many middlemen. It is likely that this more direct route helps to explain the peremptory, nearly hypnotic power some odors have over us.

a worldwide tracking system senses your EPIRB's signal and indicates its position with a blip on an electronic map. It also looks up the signature in its giant table of signatures and thereby identifies your boat. Identification greatly simplifies search and rescue, since it adds redundancy: the beacon can be homed in on blindly by radio receivers (transducers), but as the rescuers get close it helps if they know whether they are looking (with their eyes) for a black fishing trawler, a small dark-green sailboat, or a bright-orange rubber raft. Other sensory systems can be brought in to make the final approach swifter and less vulnerable to interruption (should the EPIRB's battery run down, for instance). In animals, odor tracking is not the only medium of Mamataxis. Visual and auditory signatures are also relied on, as the ethologist Konrad Lorenz has notably demonstrated in his pioneering studies of "imprinting" in young geese and ducks. Chicks that are not imprinted shortly after birth with a proper Mama signature will fix on the first large moving thing they see and treat it as Mama thereafter.

Beacons (and their complement of beacon sensors) are good design solutions whenever one agent needs to track (recognize, reidentify) a particular entity—typically another agent, such as Mama—for a long time. You just install the beacon in the target in advance, and then let it roam. (Anticar-theft radio beacons that you hide in your car and then remotely turn on if your car is stolen are a recent manifestation.) But there are costs, as usual. One of the most obvious is that friend and foe alike can use the tracking machinery to home in on the target. Predators are typically tuned to the same olfactory and auditory channels as offspring trying to stay in touch with Mama, for instance.

Odors and sounds are broadcast over a range that is not easily in the control of the emitter. A low-energy way of achieving a more selective beacon effect would be to put a particular blue spot (pigment of one sort or another) on

Mama, and let the reflected light of the sun create a beacon visible only in particular sectors of the world and readily extinguished by Mama's simply moving into the shadows. The offspring can then follow the blue spot whenever it is visible. But this setup requires an investment in more sophisticated photosensitive machinery: a simple eye, for instance—not just a pair of photocells.

The ability to stay in reliably close contact with one particular ecologically very important thing (such as Mama) does not require the ability to *conceive of* this thing as an enduring particular entity, coming and going. As we have just seen, reliable Mamataxis can be achieved with a bag of simple tricks. The talent is normally robust in simple environments, but a creature armed with such a simple system is easily "fooled," and when it is fooled, it trundles to its misfortune without any appreciation of its folly. There need be no capability for the system to monitor its own success or reflect on the conditions under which it succeeds or fails; that's a later (and expensive) add-on.

Cooperative tracking—tracking in which the target provides a handy beacon and thus simplifies the task for the tracker—is a step on the way toward competitive tracking, in which the target not only provides no unique signature beacon but actively tries to hide, to make itself untrackable. This move by prey is countered by the development in predators of general-purpose, track-anything systems, designed to turn *whatever aspects* a trackworthy thing reveals into a sort of private and temporary beacon—a "search image," created for the nonce by a gaggle of feature-detectors in the predator and used to correlate, moment by moment, the signature of the target, revising and updating the search image as the target changes, always with the goal of keeping the picked-out object in the cross-hairs.

It is important to recognize that this variety of tracking does not require categorization of the target. Think of a primitive eye, consisting of an array of a few hundred photocells, transducing a changing pattern of pixels, which are turned on by whatever is reflecting light on them. Such a system could readily deliver a message of the following sort: "*X*, the whatever-it-is responsible for the pixel-clump currently under investigation, has just dodged to the right." (It would not have to deliver this message in so many words—there need be no words, no symbols, in the system at all.) So the only identification such a system engages in is a degenerate or minimal sort of moment-to-moment reidentification of the something-or-other being tracked. Even here, there is tolerance for change and substitution. A gradually changing clump of pixels moving against a more or less static background can change its shape and internal character radically and still be trackable, so long as it doesn't change too fast. (The *phi phenomenon*, in which sequences of flashing lights are involuntarily interpreted by the vision system to be the trajectory of a moving object, is a vivid manifestation of this built-in circuitry in our own vision systems.)

What happens when *X* temporarily goes behind a tree? The simpleminded solution is to keep the most recent version of the search image intact and then just scan around at random, hoping to lock back onto this temporary beacon once again when it emerges, if it ever does. You can improve the odds by aiming your search image at the likeliest spot for the reappearance of the temporary beacon. And you can get a better-than-a-coin-flip idea of the likeliest spot just by sampling the old trajectory of the beacon and plotting its future continuation in a straight line. This yields instances of producing future in one of its simplest and most ubiquitous forms, and also gives us a clear case of the arrow of intentionality poised on a nonexistent but reasonably hoped-for target.

This ability to "keep in touch with" another object (literally touching and manipulating it, if possible) is the prerequisite for high-quality perception. Visual recognition of a particular person or object, for instance, is almost impossible if the image of the object is not kept centered on the high-resolution fovea of the eye for an appreciable length of time. It takes time for all the epistemically hungry microagents to do their feeding and get organized. So the ability to maintain such a focus of information *about* a particular thing (the whatever-it-is I'm visually tracking right now) is a precondition for developing an identifying description of the thing.*

The way to maximize the likelihood of maintaining or restoring contact with an entity being tracked is to rely on multiple independent systems, each fallible but with overlapping domains of competence. Where one system lets down the side, the others take over, and the result tends to

········

*This point about the primacy of tracking over description is, I think, the glimmer of truth in the otherwise forlorn philosophical doctrine that there are two varieties of belief—*de re* beliefs, which are somehow "directly" about their objects, and *de dicto* beliefs, which are about their objects only through the mediation of a *dictum*, a definite description (in a natural language, or in some "language of thought"). The contrast is illustrated (supposedly) by the difference between

believing that Tom (*that guy*, right over there) is a man,

and

believing that whoever it was that mailed this anonymous letter to me is a man.

The intentionality in the first case is supposed to be somehow more direct, to latch onto its object in a more primitive way. But, as we have seen, we can recast even in the most direct and primitive cases of perceptual tracking into the *de dicto* mode (the x such that x is whatever is responsible for the pixel-clump currently under investigation has just jumped to the right) in order to bring out a feature of the mechanism that mediates this most "immediate" sort of reference. The difference between *de re* and *de dicto* is a difference in the speaker's perspective or emphasis, not in the phenomenon. For more on this, see Dennett, "Beyond Belief" (1982).

be smooth and continuous tracking composed of intermittently functioning elements.

How are these multiple systems linked together? There are many possibilities. If you have two sensory systems, you can link them by means of an AND-gate: they both have to be turned ON by their input for the agent to respond positively. (An AND-gate can be implemented in any medium; it isn't a thing, but a principle of organization. The two keys that have to be turned to open a safe deposit box, or fire a nuclear missile, are linked by an AND-gate. When you fasten a garden hose to a spigot and put a controllable nozzle on the other end, these ON-OFF valves are linked by an AND-gate; both have to be open for water to come out.) Alternatively, you can link two sensory systems with an OR-gate: either one by itself, A *or* B (*or* both together), will evoke a positive response from the agent. OR-gates are used to include backup or spare subsystems in larger systems: if one unit fails, the extra unit's activity is enough to keep the system going. Twin-engined planes link their engines by an OR-gate: two in working order may be best, but in a pinch, one is enough.

As you add more systems, the possibility of linking them in intermediate ways looms. For instance, you can link them so that IF system A is ON, then if *either* B or C is ON, the system is to respond positively; otherwise, *both* systems B and C must be on to produce a positive response. (This is equivalent to a majority rule linking the three systems; if the majority—any majority—is ON, the system will respond positively.) All the possible ways of linking systems with AND-gates and OR-gates (and NOT-gates, which simply reverse or invert the output of a system, turning ON to OFF and vice versa) are called Boolean functions of those systems, since they can be precisely described in terms of the logical operators AND, OR, and NOT, which the nineteenth-century English mathematician George Boole first formalized. But there are also non-Boolean ways that systems can intermingle their effects. Instead of bringing all the contributors to a central voting place, giving them each a single vote (YES or NO, ON or OFF), and thereby channeling their contribution to behavior into a single vulnerable decision point (the summed effect of all the Boolean connections), we could let them maintain their own independent and continuously variable links to behavior and have the world extract an outcome behavior as the result of all the activity. Valentino Braitenberg's vehicle, with its two cross-wired phototransducers, is an utterly simple case in point. The "decision" to turn left or right emerges from the relative strength of the contributions of the two transducer-motor systems, but the effect is not efficiently or usefully represented as a Boolean function of the respective "arguments" of the transducers. (In principle, the input-output behavior of any such system can be approximated by a Boolean function of its components, suitably analyzed, but such an analytic stunt may fail to reveal what is important about the relationships. Considering the weather as a Boolean system is possible in principle, for instance, but unworkable and uninformative.)

By installing dozens or hundreds or thousands of such circuits in a single organism, elaborate life-protecting activities can be reliably controlled, all without anything happening inside the organism that looks like *thinking specific thoughts*. There is plenty of *as if* decision making, *as if* recognizing, *as if* hiding and seeking. There are also lots of ways an organism, so equipped, can "make mistakes," but its mistakes never amount to formulating a representation of some false proposition and then deeming it true.

How versatile can such an architecture be? It is hard to say. Researchers have recently designed and test-driven artificial control systems that produce many of the striking behavioral patterns we observe in relatively simple life-forms, such as insects and other invertebrates; so it is tempting to believe that all the astonishingly complex routines of these creatures can be orchestrated by an architecture like this, even if we don't yet know how to design a system of the required complexity. After all, the brain of an insect may have only a few hundred neurons in it, and think of the elaborate engagements with the world such an arrangement can oversee. The evolutionary biologist Robert Trivers notes, for example:

> Fungus-growing ants engage in agriculture. Workers cut leaves, carry these into the nest, prepare them as a medium for growing fungus, plant fungus on them, fertilize the fungus with their own droppings, weed out competitive species by hauling them away, and, finally, harvest a special part of the fungus on which they feed. (1985, p. 172)

Then there are the prolonged and intricately articulated mating and child-rearing rituals of fish and birds. Each step has sensory requirements that must be met before it is undertaken, and then is guided adaptively through a field of obstacles. How are these intricate maneuvers controlled? Biologists have determined many of the conditions in the environment that are used as cues, by painstakingly varying the available sources of information in experiments, but it is not enough to know what information an organism can pick up. The next difficult task is figuring out how their tiny brains can be designed to put all this useful sensitivity to information to good use.

If you are a fish or a crab or something along those lines, and one of your projects is, say, building a nest of pebbles on the ocean floor, you will need a pebble-finder device, and a way of finding your way back to *your* nest to deposit the found pebble in an appropriate place before heading out again. This system need not be foolproof, however. Since impostor pebble-nests are unlikely to be surreptitiously erected in place of your own during your foray (until clever human experimenters take an interest in you), you can keep your standards for reidentification quite low and inexpensive. If a mistake in "identification" occurs, you probably go right on building, not just taken in by the ruse but completely incapable of recognizing or appreciating the error, not in the slightest bit troubled. On the other hand, if you happen to be equipped with a backup system of nest identification, and the impostor nest fails the backup test, you will be thrown into disarray, pulled in one direction by one system and in another by the other system. These conflicts happen, but it makes no sense to ask, as the organism rushes back and forth in a tizzy, "Just what is it thinking now? What is the *propositional content* of its confused state?"

In organisms such as us—organisms equipped with many layers of self-monitoring systems, which can check on and attempt to mediate such conflicts when they arise—it can sometimes be all too clear just what mistake has been made. A disturbing example is the Capgras delusion, a bizarre affliction that occasionally strikes human beings who have suffered brain damage. The defining mark of the Capgras delusion is the sufferer's conviction that a close acquaintance (usually a loved one) has been replaced by an impostor who looks like (and sounds like, and acts like) the genuine companion, who has mysteriously disappeared! This amazing phenomenon should send shock waves through philosophy. Philosophers have made up many far-fetched cases of mistaken identity to illustrate their various philosophical theories, and the literature of philosophy is crowded with fantastic thought experiments about spies and murderers traveling incognito, best friends dressed up in gorilla suits, and long-lost identical twins, but the real-life cases of Capgras delusion have so far escaped philosophers' attention.

What is particularly surprising about these cases is that they don't depend on subtle disguises and fleeting glimpses. On the contrary, the delusion persists even when the target individual is closely scrutinized by the agent, and is even pleading for recognition. Capgras sufferers have been known to murder their spouses, so sure are they that these look-alike interlopers are trying to step into shoes—into whole lives— that are not rightfully theirs! There can be no doubt that in such a sad case, the agent in question has deemed true some very specific propositions of nonidentity: *This man is not my husband*; this man is as qualitatively similar to my husband as ever can be, and yet he is not my husband. Of particular interest to us is the fact that people suffering from such a delusion can be quite unable to say why they are so sure.

The neuropsychologist Andrew Young (1994) offers an ingenious and plausible hypothesis to explain what has gone wrong. Young contrasts Capgras delusion with another curious affliction caused by brain damage: *prosopagnosia*. People with prosopagnosia can't recognize familiar human faces. Their eyesight may be fine, but they can't identify even their closest friends until they hear them speak. In a typical experiment, they are shown collections of photographs: some photos are of anonymous individuals and others are of family members and celebrities—Hitler, Marilyn Monroe, John F. Kennedy. When asked to pick out the familiar faces, their performance is no better than chance. But for more than a decade researchers have suspected that in spite of this shockingly poor performance, *something* in some prosopagnosics was correctly identifying the family members and the famous people, since their bodies react differently to the familiar faces. If, while looking at a photo of a familiar face, they are told various candidate names of the person pictured, they show a heightened galvanic skin response when they hear the right name. (The galvanic skin response is the measure of the skin's electrical conductance and is the primary test relied on in polygraphs, or "lie detectors.") The conclusion that Young and other researchers draw from these results is that there must be two (or more) systems that can identify a face, and one of these is spared in the prosopagnosics who show this response. This system continues to do its work well, covertly and largely unnoticed. Now suppose, Young says, that Capgras sufferers have just the opposite disability: the overt, conscious face-recognition system (or systems) works just fine—which is why Capgras sufferers agree that the "impostors" do indeed look just like their loved ones—but the covert system (or systems), which normally provides a reassuring vote of agreement on such occasions, is impaired and ominously silent. The *absence* of that subtle contribution to identification is so upsetting ("Something's missing!") that it amounts to a pocket veto on the positive vote of the surviving system: the emergent result is the sufferer's heartfelt conviction that he or she is looking at an impostor. Instead of blaming the mismatch on a faulty perceptual system, the agent blames the world, in a way that is so metaphysically extravagant, so improbable, that there can be little doubt of the power (the political power, in effect) that the impaired system normally has in us all. When this particular system's epistemic hunger goes unsatisfied, it throws such a fit that it overthrows the contributions of the other systems.

In between the oblivious crab and the bizarrely mistaken Capgras sufferer there are intermediate cases. Can't a dog recognize, or fail to recognize, its master? According to Homer, when Ulysses returns to Ithaca after his twenty-year odyssey, disguised in rags as a beggar, his old dog, Argos, recognizes him, wags his tail, drops his ears, and then dies. (And Ulysses, it should be remembered, secretly wipes a tear from his own eye.) Just as there are reasons for a crab to (try to) keep track of the identity of its own nest, there are reasons for a dog to (try to) keep track of its master, among many other important things in its world. The more pressing the reasons for reidentifying things, the more it pays not to make mistakes, and hence the more investments in perceptual and cognitive machinery will pay for themselves. Advanced kinds of learning depend, in fact, on prior capacities for (re-)identification. To take a simple case, suppose a dog sees Ulysses sober on Monday, Wednesday, and Friday, but sees Ulysses drunk on Saturday. There are several conclusions that are logically available to be drawn from this set of experiences: that there are drunk men and sober men, that one man can be drunk on one day and sober on another, that Ulysses is such a man. The dog could not—logically, could not—learn the second or third fact from this sequence of separate experiences unless it had some (fallible, but relied upon) way of reidentifying the man as the same man from experience to experience. (Millikan, forthcoming) (We can see the same principle in a more dramatic application in the curious fact that you can't—as a matter of logic—learn what you look like by looking in a mirror unless you have some *other* way of identifying the face you see as yours. Without such an independent identification, you could no more discover your appearance by looking in a mirror than you could by looking at a photograph that happened to be of you.)

Dogs live in a behavioral world much richer and more complex than the world of the crab, with more opportunities for subterfuge, bluff, and disguise, and hence with more benefits to derive from the rejection of misleading clues. But again, a dog's systems need not be foolproof. If the dog makes a mistake of identification (of either sort), we can characterize it as a case of mistaken identity without yet having to conclude that the dog is capable of *thinking* the proposition which it behaves as if it believes. Argos's behavior in the story is touching, but we mustn't let sentimentality cloud our theories. Argos might also love the smells of autumn, and respond with joy each year when the first whiff of ripe fruit met his nostrils, but this would not show that he had any way of distinguishing between recurring season types, such as autumn, and returning individuals, such as Ulysses. Is Ulysses, to Argos, just an organized collection of pleasant smells and sounds, sights and feelings—a sort of irregularly recurring season (we haven't had one for twenty years!), during which particular behaviors are favored? It is a season that is usually sober, but some instances of it have been known to be drunk. *We* can see, from our peculiar human perspective, that Argos's success in this world will often depend on how closely his behavior approximates the behavior of an agent who, like us adult human beings, clearly distinguishes between individuals. So we find that when we interpret his behavior from the intentional stance, we do well to attribute beliefs to Argos that distinguish Ulysses from other people, strong rival dogs from weaker rival dogs, lambs from other animals, Ithaca from other places, and so forth. But we must be prepared to discover that this apparent understanding of his has shocking gaps in it—gaps inconceivable in a human being with our conceptual scheme, and hence utterly inexpressible in the terms of a human language.

Tales of intelligence in pets have been commonplace for millennia. The ancient Stoic philosopher Chrysippus reported a dog that could perform the following feat of reason: coming to a three-way fork, he sniffed down paths A and B, and *without sniffing* C, ran down C, having reasoned that if there is no scent down A and B, the quarry must have gone down C. People are less fond of telling tales of jaw-dropping stupidity in their pets, and often resist the implications of the gaps they discover in their pets' competences. Such a smart doggie, but can he figure out how to unwind his leash when he runs around a tree or a lamppost? This is not, it would seem, an unfair intelligence test for a dog—compared, say, with a test for sensitivity to irony in poetry, or appreciation of the transitivity of *warmer-than* (if A is warmer than B, and B is warmer than C, then A is [warmer than? colder than?] C). But few if any dogs can pass it. And dolphins, for all their intelligence, are strangely unable to figure out that they could easily leap over the surrounding tuna net to safety. Leaping out of the water is hardly an unnatural act for them, which makes their obtuseness all the more arresting. As researchers regularly discover, the more ingeniously you investigate the competence of nonhuman animals, the more likely you are to discover abrupt gaps in competence. The ability of animals to generalize from their particular exploitations of wisdom is severely limited. (For an eye-opening account of this pattern in the investigation of the minds of vervet monkeys, see Cheney and Seyfarth, *How Monkeys See the World,* 1990.)

We human beings, thanks to the perspective we gain from our ability to reflect in our special ways, can discern failures of tracking that would be quite beyond the ken of other beings. Suppose Tom has been carrying a lucky penny around for years. Tom has no name for his penny, but we shall call it Amy. Tom took Amy to Spain with him, keeps Amy on his bedside table when he sleeps, and so forth. Then one day, on a trip to New York City, Tom impulsively throws Amy into a fountain, where she blends in with the crowd of other pennies, utterly indistinguishable, by Tom and by us, from all the others—at least, all the others that have the same date of issue as Amy stamped on them. Still, Tom can *reflect* on this development. He can recognize the truth of the proposition that one, and only one, of those pennies is the lucky penny that he had always carried with him. He can be bothered (or just amused) by the fact that he has irremediably lost track of something he has been tracking, by one method or another, for years. Suppose he picks up an Amy-candidate from the fountain. He can appreciate the fact that one, and exactly one, of the following two propositions is true:

1. The penny now in my hand is the penny I brought with me to New York.
2. The penny now in my hand is not the penny I brought with me to New York.

It doesn't take a rocket scientist to appreciate that one or the other of these has to be true, even if neither Tom nor anybody else in the history of the world, past and future, can determine which. This capacity *we* have to frame, and even under most circumstances test, hypotheses about identity is quite foreign to all other creatures. The practices and projects of many creatures require them to track and reidentify individuals—their mothers, their mates, their prey, their superiors and subordinates in their band—but no evidence suggests they must appreciate that this is what they are doing when they do it. Their intentionality never rises to the pitch of metaphysical particularity that ours can rise to.

How do we do it? It doesn't take a rocket scientist to think such thoughts, but it does take a Gregorian creature who has language among its mind tools. But in order to use language, we have to be specially equipped with the talents that permit us to extract these mind tools from the (social) environment in which they reside.

. . . .

CHAPTER 5

THE CREATION OF THINKING

UNTHINKING NATURAL PSYCHOLOGISTS
. . . .

> Language was invented so that people could
> conceal their thoughts from each other.
>
> Charles-Maurice de Talleyrand

Many animals hide but don't think they are hiding. Many animals flock but don't think they are flocking. Many animals pursue, but don't think they are pursuing. They are all the beneficiaries of nervous systems that take care of the controls of these clever and appropriate behaviors without burdening the host's head with thoughts, or anything arguably like thoughts—the thoughts we thinkers think. Catching and eating, hiding and fleeing, flocking and scattering all seem to be within the competence of unthinking mechanisms. But are there clever behaviors that must be accompanied by, preceded and controlled by, clever thoughts?

If the strategy of adopting the intentional stance is as great a boon as I have claimed, then an obvious place to look for a breakthrough in animal minds is in those intentional systems who themselves are capable of adopting the intentional stance toward others (and toward themselves). We should look for behaviors that are sensitive to differences in the (hypothesized) thoughts of other animals. An old joke about behaviorists is that they don't believe in beliefs, they think that nothing can think, and in their opinion nobody has opinions. Which animals are stuck as behaviorists, unable even to entertain hypotheses about the minds of others? Which animals are forced, or enabled, to graduate to a higher level? There seems to be something paradoxical about a thoughtless agent concerning itself with the discovery and manipulation of the thoughts of other agents, so perhaps here we can find a level of sophistication that forces thinking to evolve.

Might thinking pull itself into existence by its own bootstraps? (If you're going to think about my thinking, I'm going to have to start thinking about your thinking to stay even— an arms race of reflection.) Many theorists have thought that some version of this arms race explains the evolution of higher intelligence. In an influential paper ("Nature's Psychologists," 1978), the psychologist Nicholas Humphrey argued that the development of *self*-consciousness was a stratagem for developing and testing hypotheses about what was going through the minds of *others*. It might seem that an ability to make one's behavior sensitive to, and manipulative of, the thinking of another agent would automatically carry with it an ability to make one's behavior sensitive to one's own thinking. This might be either because, as Humphrey suggested, one uses one's self-consciousness as a source of hypotheses about other-consciousness, or because when one gets into the habit of adopting the intentional stance toward others, one notices that one can usefully subject oneself to the same treatment. Or for some combination of these reasons, the habit of adopting the intentional stance could spread to cover both other-interpretation and self-interpretation.

In an essay entitled "Conditions of Personhood" (1976), I argued that an important step toward becoming a person was the step up from a *first-order* intentional system to a *second-order* intentional system. A first-order intentional system has beliefs and desires about many things, but *not* about beliefs and desires. A second-order intentional system has beliefs and desires about beliefs and desires, its own or those of others. A third-order intentional system would be capable of such feats as *wanting* you to *believe* that it *wanted* something, while a fourth-order intentional system might *believe* you *wanted* it to *believe* that you *believed* something, and so forth. The big step, I argued, was the step from first-order to second-order; the higher orders were just a matter of how much an agent can keep in its head at one time, and this varies with the circumstances, even within a single agent. Sometimes higher orders are so easy as to be involuntary. Why is the fellow in the movie trying so hard to avoid smiling? In the context it's deliciously obvious: his effort shows us he *knows* she doesn't *realize* he already *knows* she *wants* him to ask her to the dance, and he *wants* to keep it that way! Other times, simpler iterations can stump us. Are you sure that I want you to believe that I want you to believe what I'm saying here?

But if higher-order intentionality is, as I and others have argued, an important advance in kinds of minds, it is not as clearly the watershed we are looking for between thinking and unthinking cleverness. Some of the best studied examples of (apparent) higher-order intentionality among nonhuman creatures still seem to fall on the side of unreflective adroitness. Consider "distraction display," the well-known behavior of low-nesting birds, who, when a predator approaches the nest, move surreptitiously away from their vulnerable eggs or nestlings and begin in the most ostentatious way to feign a broken wing, fluttering and collapsing and calling out most piteously. This typically leads the predator far away from the nest on a wild goose chase, in which it never quite catches the "easy" dinner it is offered. The free-floating rationale of this behavior is clear, and, following Richard Dawkins's useful practice in his 1976 book, *The Selfish Gene*, we can put it in the form of an *imaginary* soliloquy:

> I'm a low-nesting bird, whose chicks are not protectable against a predator who discovers them. This approaching predator can be *expected* soon to discover them unless I distract it; it could be distracted by its *desire* to catch and eat me, but only if it *thought* there was a *reasonable* chance of its actually catching me (it's no dummy); it would contract just that *belief* if I *gave it evidence that* I couldn't fly anymore; I could do that by feigning a broken wing, etc. (From Dennett, 1983)

In the case of Brutus stabbing Caesar, discussed in chapter 2, it was within the bounds of plausibility to suppose that Brutus actually went through something like the soliloquy process outlined for him—though normally, in even the most loquacious self-addresser, much of it would go without saying. It defies credence, however, to suppose that any bird goes through anything like the soliloquy here. Yet that soliloquy undoubtedly expresses the rationale that has shaped the behavior, whether or not the bird can appreciate the rationale. Research by the ethologist Carolyn Ristau (1991) has shown that in at least one such species—the piping plover—individuals govern their distraction displays with quite sophisticated controls. For instance, they monitor the direction of the predator's gaze, turning up the volume of their display if the predator seems to be losing interest, and in other ways adapt their behavior to features detected in the predator's. Plovers also discriminate on the basis of an interloper's shape and size: since cows aren't carnivorous, a cow is not apt to be attracted by the prospect of an easy bird meal, so some plovers treat cows differently, squawking and pecking and trying to drive the beast away instead of luring it away.

Hares apparently can size up an approaching predator, such as a fox, and make an estimate of its dangerousness (Hasson, 1991, Holley, 1994). If the hare determines that a particular fox has somehow managed to get within striking distance, it will either crouch and freeze—counting on escaping the notice of the fox altogether—or crouch and scurry as swiftly and quietly as it can, ducking behind whatever cover is available. But if the hare determines that this fox is unlikely to succeed in its chase, it does a strange and wonderful thing. It stands up on its hind legs, most conspicuously, and stares the fox down! Why? Because it is announcing to the fox that the fox ought to give up. "I've already seen you, and I'm not afraid. Don't waste your precious time and even more precious energy chasing me. Give it up!" And the fox typically draws just this conclusion, turning elsewhere for its supper and leaving the hare, which has thus conserved its own energy, to continue its own feeding.

Once again, the rationale of this behavior is almost certainly free-floating. It is probably not a tactic the hare has figured out for itself, or been capable of reflecting on. Gazelles being chased by lions or hyenas often do something similar, called stotting. They make ridiculously high leaps, obviously of no benefit to their flight but designed to advertise their superior speed to the predators. "Don't bother chasing *me*. Chase my cousin. I'm so fast I can waste time and energy doing these silly leaps and still outrun you." And it apparently works; predators typically turn their attention to other animals.

Other varieties of predator and prey behavior could be cited, all with elaborate rationales but little or no evidence that the animals actually represent these rationales to themselves in any fashion. If *these* creatures are to be considered "natural psychologists" (to use Humphrey's term), they are apparently unthinking natural psychologists. These creatures don't represent the minds of those they interact with—that is, they don't need to consult any internal "model" of the mind of another in order to anticipate the other's behavior and hence govern their own behavior. They are well-supplied with a largish "list" of alternative behaviors, nicely linked to a largish list of perceptual cues, and they don't need to know any more. Does this count as mind reading? Are piping plovers, or hares, or gazelles higher-order intentional systems or not? That question begins to appear less important than the question of how such an apparent mind-reading competence might be organized. When, then, does the need arise to go beyond these large lists? The ethologist Andrew Whiten has suggested that the need arises simply when the lists get too long and unwieldy to be supplemented. Such a list of pairs amounts, in logicians' terms, to a conjunction of conditionals, or if-then pairs:

[If you see x, do A], and [if you see y, do B], and [if you see z, do C], . . .

Depending on just how many independent conditionals there are, it may become economical to consolidate them into more organized representations of the world. Perhaps in some species—which species remains an open question—the brilliant innovation of explicit *generalization* enters the picture, permitting the lists to be broken down and rebuilt on demand from first principles, as new cases arise. Consider Whiten's diagram of the complexity that would get organized around an internal representation by one animal of a specific desire in another animal.

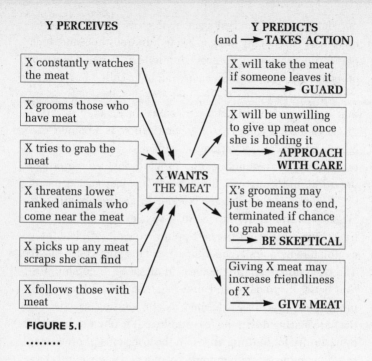

Y PERCEIVES

X constantly watches the meat

X grooms those who have meat

X tries to grab the meat

X threatens lower ranked animals who come near the meat

X picks up any meat scraps she can find

X follows those with meat

X WANTS THE MEAT

Y PREDICTS
(and ⟶ **TAKES ACTION**)

X will take the meat if someone leaves it
⟶ **GUARD**

X will be unwilling to give up meat once she is holding it
⟶ **APPROACH WITH CARE**

X's grooming may just be means to end, terminated if chance to grab meat
⟶ **BE SKEPTICAL**

Giving X meat may increase friendliness of X
⟶ **GIVE MEAT**

FIGURE 5.1
········

As before, *we* can see the rationale behind such consolidation, but this rationale need not be entertained in any fashion by the minds of the consolidators. If they are lucky enough to hit upon this design improvement, they could simply be the beneficiaries of it without appreciating why or how it worked. But is this design really the improvement it appears to be? What are its costs and benefits? And its value aside, how could it have come into existence? Did it just arise one day, in random and desperate reaction to a growing problem of "overhead"—too many conditional rules to keep in service simultaneously? Perhaps, but nobody yet knows any plausible upper bound on the number of concurrent semi-independent control structures that can coexist in a nervous system. (In a real agent with a real nervous system, there may not be any. Maybe a few hundred thousand such perceptuo-behavioral control circuits can mingle together efficiently in a brain—how many might be called for?)

Might there not be some other sort of selective pressure that could have led to the reorganization of control structures, yielding a capacity for generalization as a bonus? The ethologist David McFarland (1989) has argued that the opportunity for communication provides just such a design pressure, and moreover, Talleyrand's cynical suggestion at the opening of this chapter is close to an important truth. When communication arises in a species, he claims, pure honesty is clearly not the best policy, since it will be all too exploitable by one's competitors (Dawkins and Krebs, 1978). The competitive context is clear in all cases of communication between predator and prey, such as the minimal communication practices exhibited by the stotting gazelle and the hare staring down the fox; and here it is obvious how the opportunity for bluffing arises. In the arms race of producing future, you have a tremendous advantage if you can produce more and better future about the other than the other can produce about you, so it always behooves an agent to keep its own control system inscrutable. Unpredictability is in general a fine protective feature, which should never be squandered but always spent wisely. There is much to be gained from communication if it is craftily doled out—enough truth to keep one's credibility high but enough falsehood to keep one's options open. (This is the first point of wisdom in the game of poker: he who never bluffs never wins; he who always bluffs always loses.) It takes some stretching of the imagination to see the hare and fox as cooperating on their joint problems of resource management, but in fact they are both better off for their occasional truces.

The prospects for expanding cooperation and hence multiplying its benefits is much more clearly visible in the context of communication with members of one's own species. Here food sharing, and sharing the costs and risks of child care and defense of the group, and so forth, provide plenty of opportunities for cooperation, but only if the rather stringent conditions for exploiting these opportunities can be met. Cooperation between parents, or between parents and offspring, cannot be taken as a given in nature; the omnipresent possibility of competition still lies behind any mutually useful conventions that emerge, and this context of competition must be taken into account.

According to McFarland, the need for an explicit, manipulable representation of one's behavior arises only when the option of potentially cooperative but still self-protective communication emerges, for then a new form of behavior must come under the agent's control: the behavior of explicitly communicating something about one's other behavior. ("I'm trying to catch fish," or "I'm looking for my mother," or "I'm just resting.") Confronted with the task of shaping and executing such a communicative act, the agent's problem is a version of the very problem confronting us as observing theorists: How should the agent's own tangle of competing, enhancing, merging, intertwining behavioral control circuits be carved up into competing "alternatives"? Communication favors clear-cut answers. As the saying goes, "Are you going to fish or cut bait?" So the demands of communication, by forcing an agent into declaring a category, may often create a distortion—rather like the distortion you recognize when required to check off just one item in a poorly designed multiple-choice test: if "none of the above" is not an available option, you are forced to settle for whatever you take to be the least objectionable near miss. McFarland suggests that this task of carving where nature has provided no salient joints is a problem the agent solves by what we might call *approximating confabulation*. The agent comes to label its tendencies *as if* they were governed by explicitly represented goals—blueprints for actions—instead of trends of action that emerge from the interplay of the various candidates. Once such *representations of intentions* (in the everyday sense of intentions) come into existence in this backhanded way, they may succeed in convincing the agent itself that it has these clear-cut prior intentions governing its actions. In order to solve its communication problem, the agent has made a special user-interface for itself, a menu of explicit options from which to choose, and then has been to some degree taken in by its own creation.

Opportunities to put such communications to good use are strictly limited, however. Many environments are inhospitable to secret keeping, quite independently of any proclivities or talents of the agents in that environment; and if you can't keep a secret there is little role for communication to play. According to ancient folk wisdom, people who live in glass houses shouldn't throw stones, but animals who live in the natural equivalent of glass houses have no stones to throw. Animals who live close together in groups in open territory are seldom if ever out of sight and hearing (and smell and touch) of their conspecifics for very long, and thus have no opportunities to satisfy the conditions under which secrets can flourish. Suppose that p is an ecologically valuable fact, and suppose that you know that p and nobody else does—yet. If you and the other potentially competitive agents in the vicinity all have access to pretty much the same information about the environment, then it is next to impossible for circumstances to arise in which you can turn such a temporary information-gradient to your advantage. You may be the first wildebeest to see or smell the lion to the northwest, but you can't really hoard (or sell) this information, because those standing shoulder to shoulder with you will soon have it themselves. Since there is scant possibility that such a temporary information advantage can be controlled, a devious wildebeest (for example) would have precious little opportunity to benefit from its talent. Just what could it do to gain sneaky advantage over the others?

The intentional stance shows us readily that the apparently simple behavior of *keeping a secret*—a null behavior, from most vantage points—is in fact a behavior whose success depends on satisfying a rather demanding set of conditions. Suppose that *Bill is keeping some secret, p, from Jim.* The following conditions must be met:

1. Bill knows (believes) that p.
2. Bill believes that Jim does not believe that p.
3. Bill wants Jim not to come to believe that p.
4. Bill believes that Bill can make it the case that Jim not come to believe that p.

It is this last condition that restricts advanced secret-keeping (for instance, about features of the external environment) to quite specific behavioral environments. This was clearly brought out by experiments in the 1970s by the primatologist Emil Menzel (1971, 1974), in which individual chimpanzees were shown the location of hidden food, and thereby given the opportunity to deceive the other chimpanzees about its location. They often rose to the opportunity, with fascinating results, but this behavior always depended on the experimenters' producing a state of affairs in the laboratory (a cage adjacent to a larger fenced enclosure, in this case) that would only rarely occur in the wild: the chimpanzee who sees the hidden food must be in a position to *know that the other chimpanzees do not see him seeing the food.* This was achieved by keeping all the other chimpanzees locked in a common cage while the chosen chimpanzee was taken alone into the larger enclosure and shown the hidden food. The chosen chimpanzee could come to learn that it alone was learning that p—that its informative adventures in the enclosure were not visible to the others in the cage. And, of course, there had to be something the chimp with the secret could do to protect its secret—at least, for a while—once the others were released.

Chimpanzees in the wild do frequently wander far enough away from their groups for long enough to acquire secrets within their control, so they are a good species to examine with such tests. In animals whose evolutionary history has not unfolded in environments in which such opportunities naturally and frequently arise, there is little likelihood that the capacity to exploit such opportunities has evolved. Discovering (in the lab) a heretofore unused talent is not impossible, of course, since unused talent must surface, rarely, in the real world, whenever innovation occurs. Such a talent will typically be a by-product of other talents developed under other selection pressures. In general, however, since we expect cognitive complexity to coevolve with environmental complexity, we should look for cognitive complexity first in those species that have a long history of dealing with the relevant sort of environmental complexity.

Taken together, these points *suggest* that thinking—our kind of thinking—had to wait for talking to emerge, which in turn had to wait for secret keeping to emerge, which in turn had to wait for the right complexification of the behavioral environment. We should be surprised to find thinking in any species that hasn't made it to the bottom of this cascade of sieves. As long as the behavioral options are relatively simple—witness the piping plover's predicament—no fancy central representation needs to occur, so in all likelihood it doesn't. The sort of higher-order sensitivity required to meet the needs of a piping plover or a hare or a gazelle can probably be provided by networks designed almost entirely by Darwinian mechanisms, abetted here and there by Skinnerian mechanisms. ABC learning, then, could probably suffice to produce such a sensitivity—though this is an empirical issue that is nowhere near settled. It will be interesting to discover if there are cases in which we have clear evidence of differential treatment of specific *individuals* (a piping plover that doesn't waste its ruses on a particular reidentified dog, say, or a hare that, after a particular close call, drastically increases its stare-down distance for a specific fox.) Even in these cases, we *may* be able to account for the learning via relatively simple models: these animals are Popperian creatures—creatures who can be guided by past experience to reject tempting but untested candidates for action—but still not explicit thinkers.

As long as the natural psychologists don't have an opportunity or an obligation to communicate with each other about their attributions of intentionality to themselves or others, as long as they never have an opportunity to compare notes, to dispute with others, to *ask for the reasons* that ground the conclusions they are curious about, it seems that there is no selective pressure on them to represent those reasons, and hence no selective pressure on them to forsake the Need to Know principle in favor of its familiar opposite, the Commando Team Principle: give each agent as much knowledge about the total project as possible, so that the team has a chance of ad-libbing appropriately when unanticipated obstacles arise. (Many films, such as *The Guns of Navarone*, or *The Dirty Dozen*, make this principle visible by presenting the exploits of such versatile and knowing teams; hence my name for it.)

The free-floating rationales that explain the rudimentary higher-order intentionality of birds and hares—and even chimpanzees—are honored in the designs of their nervous systems, but we are looking for something more; we are looking for rationales that are *represented* in those nervous systems.

Although ABC learning can yield remarkably subtle and powerful discriminatory competences, capable of teasing out the patterns lurking in voluminous arrays of data, these competences tend to be anchored in the specific tissues that are modified by training. They are "embedded" competences, in the sense that they are incapable of being "transported" readily to be brought to bear on other problems faced by the individual, or shared with other individuals. The philosopher Andy Clark and the psychologist Annette Karmiloff-Smith (1993) have recently been exploring the transition from a brain that has only such embedded knowledge to a brain that, as they say, "enriches itself from within by re-representing the knowledge that it has already represented." Clark and Karmiloff-Smith note that while there are clear benefits to a design policy that "intricately interweave[s] the various aspects of our knowledge about a domain in a single knowledge structure," there are costs as well: "The interweaving makes it practically impossible to operate on or otherwise exploit the various dimensions of our knowledge independently of one another." So opaquely is such knowledge hidden in the mesh of the connections that "it is knowledge *in* the system, but it is not yet knowledge *to* the system"—like the wisdom revealed in the precocious single-mindedness with which the newly hatched cuckoo shoulders the competing eggs out of the nest. What would have to be added to the cuckoo's computational architecture for it to be able to appreciate, understand, and exploit the wisdom interwoven in its neural nets?

A popular answer to this question, in its many guises, is "symbols!" The answer is well-nigh tautological, and hence is bound to be right in *some* interpretation. How could it not be the case that implicit or tacit knowledge becomes explicit by being expressed or rendered in some medium of "explicit" representation? Symbols, unlike the nodes woven into connectionist networks, are movable; they can be manipulated; they can be composed into larger structures, in which their contribution to the meaning of the whole can be a definite and generatable function of the structure—the syntactic structure—of the parts. There is surely something right about this, but we must proceed cautiously, since many pioneers have posed these questions in ways that have turned out to be misleading.

We human beings have the capacity for swift, insightful learning—learning that does not depend on laborious training but is ours as soon as we contemplate a suitable symbolic representation of the knowledge. When psychologists devise a new experimental setup or paradigm in which to test such nonhuman subjects as rats or cats or monkeys or dolphins, they often have to devote dozens or even hundreds of hours to training each subject on the new tasks. Human subjects, however, can usually just be told what is desired of them. After a brief question-and-answer session and a few minutes of practice, we human subjects will typically be as competent in the new environment as any agent ever could be. Of course, we do have to *understand* the representations that are presented to us in these tests, and that's where the transition from ABC learning to our kind of learning is still shrouded in fog. An insight that may help clear it is a familiar maxim of artifact making: if you "do it yourself," you understand it. To anchor a free-floating rationale to an agent in the strong way, so that it is *the agent's own* reason, the agent must "make" something. A representation of the reason must be composed, designed, edited, revised, manipulated, endorsed. How does any agent come to be able to do such a wonderful thing? Does it have to grow a new organ in its brain? Or can it build this competence out of the sorts of external-world manipulations it has already mastered?

MAKING THINGS TO THINK WITH
········

> Just as you cannot do very much carpentry with
> your bare hands, there is not much thinking you
> can do with your bare brain.
>
> Bo Dahlbom and Lars-Erik Janlert,
> *Computer Future* (forthcoming)

Every agent faces the task of making the best use of its environment. The environment contains a variety of goods and toxins, mixed in with a confusing host of more indirect clues: harbingers and distractors, stepping-stones and pitfalls. These resources often amount to an embarrassment of riches in competition for the agent's attention; the agent's task of resource management (and refinement) is thus one in which time is a crucial dimension. Time spent in a futile pursuit of prey, or bracing oneself to withstand illusory threats, is time wasted, and time is precious.

As suggested in figure 4.4, Gregorian creatures take in from the environment various designed entities and use them to improve the efficiency and accuracy of their hypothesis testing and decision making, but the diagram is misleading as it stands. How much room is there in the brain for these artifacts, and how do they get installed? Is the brain of a Gregorian creature so much more capacious than the brains of other creatures? Our brains are modestly larger than the brains of our nearest relatives (although not larger than the brains of some dolphins and whales), but this is almost certainly not the source of our greater intelligence. The primary source, I want to suggest, is our habit of *offloading* as much as possible of our cognitive tasks into the environment itself—extruding our minds (that is, our mental projects and activities) into the surrounding world, where a host of peripheral devices we construct can store, process, and re-represent our meanings, streamlining, enhancing, and protecting the processes of transformation that *are* our thinking. This widespread practice of off-loading releases us from the limitations of our animal brains.

An agent faces its environment with its current repertoire of skills, perceptual and behavioral. If the environment is too complicated for these skills to cope, the agent is in trouble unless it can develop new skills, or simplify its environment. Or both. Most species rely on natural landmarks to find their way around, and some species have developed the trick of adding landmarks to the world for their subsequent use. Ants, for instance, lay down pheromone trails—odor trails—leading from nest to food and back, and the individuals in many territorial species mark the boundaries of their territories with idiosyncratic aromatic compounds in their urine. Posting your land in this way warns off trespassers, but it also provides a handy device you can use yourself. It saves you from needing some other way to remember the boundary of that part of the environment in which you have invested significant efforts of resource refinement—or even cultivation. As you approach the boundary, you can smell it. You let the outside world store some easily transduced information about where the important joints in nature are, so that you can save your limited brain for other things. This is good stewardship. Putting deliberate marks on the environment to use in distinguishing what are for you its most important features is an excellent way of reducing the cognitive load on your perception and memory. It's a variation on, and enhancement of, evolution's good tactic of installing beacons where most needed.

For us human beings, the benefits of labeling things in our environments are so obvious that we tend to overlook the rationale of labeling, and the conditions under which it works. Why does anyone ever label anything, and what does it take to label something? Suppose you were searching through thousands of boxes of shoes, looking for a house key that you thought was hidden in one of them. Unless you're an idiot, or so frantic in your quest that you cannot pause to consider the wisest course, you will devise some handy scheme for getting the environment to assist you with your problem. You want in particular to avoid wasting time by looking more than once in each box. One way would be to move the boxes one at a time from one stack (the unexamined stack) to another stack (the examined stack). Another way, potentially more energy efficient, is to put a check mark on each box as you examine it, and then adopt the rule of never looking into a box with a check mark on it. A check mark makes the world simpler, by giving you a simple perceptual task in place of a more difficult—perhaps impossible—memory and recognition task. Notice that if the boxes are all lined up in a row, and you don't have to worry about unnoticed reorderings of the queue, you don't need to put check marks on them; you can just work your way from left to right, using the simple distinguisher that nature has already provided you with—the left/right distinction.

Now let's concentrate on the check mark itself. Will *anything* do as a check mark? Clearly not. "I'll put a faint smudge somewhere on each box as I examine it." "I'll bump the corner of each box as I examine it." Not good choices, since the likelihood is too high that something else may already have inadvertently put such a mark on a box. You need something distinctive, something that you can be confident is the result of your labeling act and not some extraneously produced blemish. It should also be memorable, of course, so that you won't be beset by confusions about whether or not some salient label you encounter is a label *you* put there, and if so, what policy you meant to follow when you adopted it. There's no use tying a string around your finger as a reminder if, when it later *catches your eye* (thereby fulfilling its function as a self-control beacon off-loaded into the environment), you can't remember why you tied it. Such simple deliberate marks on the world are the most primitive precursors of writing, a step toward the creation in the external world of dedicated peripheral information-storage systems. Notice that this innovation does not depend on there being a systematic language in which such labels are composed. Any nonce system will do, as long as it can be remembered during use.

Which species have discovered these strategies? Some recent experiments give us a tantalizing, if inconclusive, glimpse into the possibilities. Birds that hide caches of seeds at many specific locations are astonishingly successful at retrieving their secret stores after long intervals. Clark's nutcrackers, for instance, have been experimentally studied by the biologist Russell Balda and his colleagues in an enclosed laboratory setting—a large room with either a dirt floor or a floor provided with many holes filled with sand, and further furnished with various landmarks. The birds may make more than a dozen caches with seeds provided to them, and then return, days later, to recover them. They are remarkably good at relying on multiple cues, finding most of their caches even when the experimenters move or remove some of the landmarks. But they do make mistakes in the laboratory, and most of these mistakes seem to be errors of self-control: they waste time and energy by revisiting sites they have already cleaned out on earlier expeditions. Since these birds may make several thousand caches in the wild, and visit them over a period of more than six months, the frequency of such wasted revisits in the wild is almost impossible to record, but it stands to reason that revisiting would be a costly habit to fall into, and other species of caching birds, such as chickadees, are known to be able to avoid such revisits.

In the wild, Clark's nutcrackers are observed to eat the seeds where they dig them up, leaving behind a mess of picnic litter that could remind them, on another fly-by, that they had already opened that particular shoebox. Balda and his colleagues designed experiments to test the hypothesis that the birds relied on such marks to avoid revisits. In one condition, the birds' disturbances of the visited sites were carefully erased between sessions, and in another the telltale disturbances were left. In this laboratory setting, however, the birds did not do significantly better when the disturbances were left, so it has not been shown that the birds do rely on these cues. Perhaps they couldn't in the wild, since such cues are often soon obliterated by weather in any case, as Balda notes. He also points out that the experiments to date are inconclusive; the cost of error in the laboratory setting is slight—a few seconds wasted in the life of a well-fed bird.

It is also possible that putting the birds in a laboratory setting inadvertently renders them relatively incompetent, since their everyday habits of distributing part of the task of self-control to the environment may depend on further cues that are inadvertently absent in the laboratory. It is commonly observed—but not commonly enough!—that old folks removed from their homes to hospital settings are put at a tremendous disadvantage, even though their basic bodily needs are well provided for. They often *appear* to be quite demented—to be utterly incapable of feeding, clothing, and washing themselves, let alone engaging in any activities of greater interest. Often, however, if they are returned to their homes, they can manage quite well for themselves. How do they do this? Over the years, they have loaded their home environments with ultrafamiliar landmarks, triggers for habits, reminders of what to do, where to find the food, how to get dressed, where the telephone is, and so forth. An old person can be a veritable virtuoso of self-help in such a hugely overlearned world, in spite of his or her brain's increasing imperviousness to new bouts of learning—of the ABC variety or any other. Taking them out of their homes is literally separating them from large parts of their minds—potentially just as devastating a development as undergoing brain surgery.

Perhaps some birds unthinkingly make check marks as a by-product of their other activities. We human beings certainly rely on many check marks unwittingly placed in our surroundings. We pick up helpful habits that we vaguely appreciate without ever stopping to understand why they're such treasures. Think of trying to do multidigit multiplication problems in your head. How much is 217 times 436? No one would try to answer this without the help of pencil and paper, except as a stunt. The tally on paper serves more than one useful function; it provides a reliable store for the intermediate results, but the individual symbols also serve as landmarks that can be followed, reminding you, as your eyes and fingers reach each point, of what the next step in the overlearned recipe should be. (If you doubt the second contribution, just try doing multidigit multiplication in which you write down the intermediate results on separate slips of paper placed in a nonstandard arrangement in front of you, instead of lining them up in the canonical way.) We Gregorian creatures are the beneficiaries of literally thousands of such useful technologies, invented by others in the dim recesses of history or prehistory but transmitted via cultural highways, not via the genetic pathways of inheritance. We learn, thanks to this cultural heritage, how to spread our minds out in the world, where we can put our beautifully designed innate tracking and pattern-recognizing talents to optimal use.

Making such a change in the world doesn't just take a load off memory. It may also permit the agent to bring to bear some cognitive talent that otherwise would be underutilized, by preparing special materials for it—in the minimal case, unwittingly. The roboticist Philippe Gaussier (1994) has recently provided a vivid illustration of this possibility, using tiny robots that first alter their environment and then have their own behavioral repertoire altered in turn by the new environment they have created. These robots are real-world Braitenberg vehicles—called *Kheperas* (the Italian word for scarab beetles) by their creator, the roboticist Francesco Mondada. They are somewhat smaller than hockey pucks, and they roll around on two tiny wheels and a castor. The robots have extremely rudimentary visual systems—just two or three photocells—connected to their wheels in such a way that signals from them turn the robots away from collisions with the walls that surround their tabletop world. So these robots are innately equipped, you might say, with a visually guided wall-avoidance system. Small, movable "pegs"—little cylinders of wood—are scattered about on the tabletop, and the robots' innate vision systems cause them to duck around these lightweight obstacles too, but wire hooks on their backs typically snag the pegs as the robots go by. They scurry around in random walks on the tabletop, unwittingly picking up pegs and then depositing them whenever they swerve sharply in the direction of a carried peg. (See figure 5.2) Over time, these encounters redistribute the pegs in the environment, and whenever two or more pegs happen to be deposited next to each other, they form a group that the robots subsequently "misperceive" as a bit of wall—to be avoided. In short order, and without further instruction from any Central Headquarters, the robots will line up all the pegs that have been scattered in their environment, organizing their environment into a series of connected walls. The Kheperas' random walks in an initially random environment first structure that environment into something like a maze, and then use that structure to shape their own behavior; they become wall followers.

This is as simple a case as can be imagined of a tactic that includes, at the sophisticated end of the spectrum, all dia-

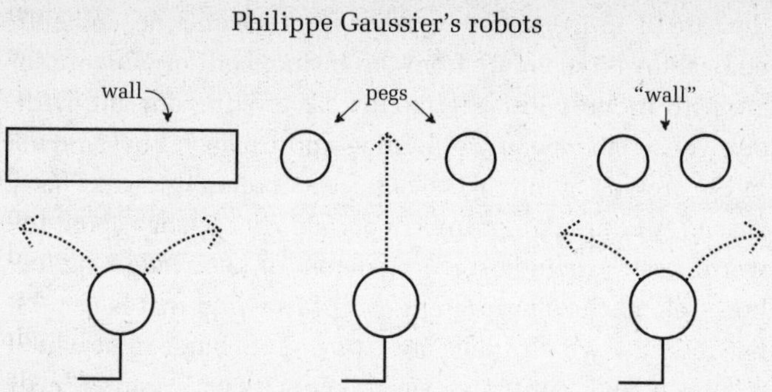

Philippe Gaussier's robots

FIGURE 5.2
·······

gram drawing and model building. Why do we ever draw a diagram—for instance, on a blackboard or (in earlier days) on the floor of the cave with a sharp stick? We do so because by re-representing the information in another format, we make it presentable to one special-purpose perceptual competence or another.

Popperian creatures—and their subvariety, the Gregorian creatures—live in an environment that can be roughly divided into two parts: the "external" and the "internal." The denizens of the "internal" environment are distinguished not so much by which side of the skin they are found on (as B. F. Skinner has remarked [1964, p. 84], "The skin is not that important as a boundary") as by whether they're portable, and hence largely omnipresent, and hence relatively more controllable and better known, and hence more likely to be designed for an agent's benefit. (As we noted in chapter 2, the shopping list on the slip of paper gets its meaning in exactly the same way as a shopping list memorized in the brain.) The "external" environment changes in many hard-to-track ways, and is, in the main, geographically outside the creature. (The limits of geography in drawing this distinction are nowhere more vividly illustrated than in the case of antigens, evil invaders from the outside, and anti-bodies, loyal defenders from the inside, both of which mingle with friendly forces—like the bacteria in your gut, without whose labors you would die—and irrelevant bystanders, in the crowds of microbe-sized agents populating your body space.) A Popperian creature's portable knowledge about the world has to include some modicum of knowledge—know-how—about the omnipresent part of its world that is *itself*. It has to know which limbs are its own, of course, and which mouth to feed, but it also has to know its way around in its own brain, to some extent. And how does it do that? By using the same old methods: by placing landmarks and labels wherever they would come in handy! Among the resources to be managed under time pressure by an agent are the resources of its own nervous system. This self-knowledge need not itself be represented explicitly, any more than the wisdom of an unthinking creature needs to be represented explicitly. It can be mere embedded know-how, but it is crucial know-how about how to manipulate that curiously docile and relatively unfleeting part of the world that is oneself.

You want these refinements of your internal resources to simplify your life, so that you can do more things better and do them faster—time is *always* precious—with your available repertoire of talents. Once again, there is no use creating an *internal* symbol as a tool to use in self-control if when it "catches your mind's eye" you can't remember why you created it. The manipulability of any system of pointers, landmarks, labels, symbols, and other reminders depends on the underlying robustness of your native talents at tracking and reidentification, providing you with redundant, multimodal paths of accessibility to your tools. The resource management techniques you are born with make no distinction between interior and exterior things. In Gregorian creatures, such as us, the representations of features and things in the (external *or* internal) world become objects in their own right—things to be manipulated, tracked, moved, hoarded, lined up, studied, turned upside down, and otherwise adjusted and exploited.

In her book *On Photography* (1977), the literary critic Susan Sontag points out that the advent of high-speed still photography was a revolutionary technological advance for science because it permitted human beings, for the first time ever, to examine complicated temporal phenomena not in real time but *in their own good time*—in leisurely, methodical, backtracking analysis of the traces they had created of those complicated events. As noted in chapter 3, our natural minds are equipped to deal with changes that occur only at particular paces. Events that happen faster or slower are simply invisible to us. Photography was a technological advance that carried in its wake a huge enhancement in cognitive power, by permitting us to re-represent the events of interest in the world in a format, and at a rate, that was tailor-made for our particular senses.

Before there were cameras and high-speed film, there were plenty of observational and recording devices that permitted the scientist to extract data precisely from the world for subsequent analysis at his leisure. The exquisite diagrams and illustrations of several centuries of science are testimony to the power of these methods, but there is something special about a camera: it is "stupid." In order to "capture" the data represented in its products, it does not have to understand its subject in the way a human artist or illustrator must. It thus passes along an unedited, uncontaminated, unbiased but still re-represented version of reality to the faculties that are equipped to analyze, and ultimately understand, the phenomena. This mindless mapping of complex data into simpler, more natural or user-friendly formats is, as we have seen, a hallmark of increasing intelligence.

But along with the camera, and the huge pile of still photographs that poured out of it, came a resource problem: the photos themselves needed to be labeled. It does scant good to capture an event of interest in a still picture, if you can't remember which of thousands of prints lying around the office is the one that represents the event of interest. This "matching problem" doesn't arise for simpler, more direct varieties of tracking, as we have seen, but the cost of solving it should often be borne; the trick can pay for itself (time is money) in cases in which it permits indirect tracking of important things that cannot be tracked directly. Think of the brilliant practice of sticking colored pins in a map to mark the location of each of a large number of events we are trying to understand. An epidemic may be diagnosed by see-ing—*seeing*, thanks to color coding—that all the cases of one sort line up on the map alongside one or another inconspic-uous or even heretofore undepicted feature—the water main, or the sewage system, or perhaps the route of the postman. A serial killer's secret base of operations may sometimes be homed in on—a variety of villaintaxis—by plotting the geo-graphic center of the cluster of his attacks. The dramatic improvements in all our kinds of investigations, from the foraging strategies of our hunter-gatherer days to the contem-porary investigations by our police, poetry critics, and physicists, are due in the main to the explosive growth in our technologies of re-representation.

We keep "pointers" and "indices" in our brains and leave as much of the actual data as we can in the external world, in our address books, libraries, notebooks, computers—and, indeed, in our circle of friends and associates. A human mind is not only not limited to the brain but would be rather severely disabled if these external tools were removed—at least as disabled as the near-sighted are when their eye-glasses are taken away. The more data and devices you off-load, the more dependent you become on these peripherals; nevertheless, the more intimately familiar you become with the peripheral objects thanks to your practice in manipulating them, the more confidently you can then do without them, sucking the problems back into your head and solving them in an imagination disciplined by its external practice. (Can you alphabetize the words in this sentence in your head?)

A particularly rich source of new techniques of re-representation is the habit that we—and only we—have developed of deliberately mapping our new problems onto our old problem-solving machinery. Consider, for instance, the many different methods we have developed for thinking about time by actually thinking about space (Jaynes, 1976). We have all sorts of conventional ways of mapping past, present, and future, before and after, sooner and later—differences that are virtually invisible in unrefined nature—onto left and right, up and down, clockwise and counterclockwise. Monday is to the left of Tuesday for most of us, while (in a valuable convention that is fading from our culture, sad to say) four o'clock is tucked under three o'clock on the right hand side of every day or night. Our spatialization of time doesn't stop there. In science, particularly, it extends to graphs, which have by now become a familiar system of diagrams for almost all literate people. (Think of the profits, or the temperature, or the loudness of your stereo, rising up up up from left to right with the passage of time.) We use our sense of space to *see* the passage of time (usually from left to right, in standard convention, except in evolutionary diagrams, in which earlier eras are often shown at the bottom, with *today* at the top). As these examples show—the absence of any figures in the text at this point is deliberate—our ability to *imagine* these diagrams when verbally invited to do so is itself a valuable Gregorian competence, with many uses. Our ability to imagine these diagrams is parasitic on our ability to draw and see them, off-loading them at least temporarily into the external world.

Thanks to our prosthetically enhanced imaginations, we can formulate otherwise imponderable, unnoticeable metaphysical possibilities, such as the case of Amy the lucky penny, discussed at the end of chapter 4. We need to be able to imagine the otherwise invisible trajectory line linking the genuine Amy of yesterday with just one of the look-alike pennies in the pile—we need to draw it "in our mind's eye." Without such visual aids, internal or external, we would have great difficulty following, let alone contributing to, these metaphysical observations. (Does that mean that someone born blind couldn't participate in such metaphysical discussions? No, because the blind develop their own methods of spatial imagining, concerned, just as a sighted person's imagining is, with keeping track of moving things in space, one way or another. But an interesting question is what differences, if any, can be found in the styles of abstract thinking adopted by those born blind or deaf.) Armed with these mind tools, we tend to forget that *our* ways of thinking about the world are not the only ways, and in particular are not prerequisites for engaging the world successfully. It probably seems obvious, at first, that since they are so manifestly intelligent, dogs and dolphins and bats must have concepts more or less like ours, but on reflection it shouldn't seem obvious at all. Most of the questions we've raised from our evolutionary perspective about the ontology and epistemology of other creatures have not yet been answered, and the answers will no doubt be surprising. We have taken only the first step: we've seen some possibilities to be investigated that we overlooked before.

Of all the mind tools we acquire in the course of furnishing our brains from the stockpiles of culture, none are more important, of course, than words—first spoken, then written. Words make us more intelligent by making cognition easier, in the same way (many times multiplied) that beacons and landmarks make navigation in the world easier for simple creatures. Navigation in the abstract multidimensional world of ideas is simply impossible without a huge stock of movable, memorable landmarks that can be shared, criticized, recorded, and looked at from different perspectives. It's important to remember that speaking and writing are two entirely distinct innovations, separated by many hundreds of thousands (and maybe millions) of years, and that each has its own distinct set of powers. We tend to run the two phenomena together, especially when theorizing about the brain or mind. Most of what has been written about the possibilities of a "language of thought" as a medium of cognitive operations presupposes that we're thinking of a *written* language of thought—"brain writing and mind reading," as I put it some years ago. We can get a better perspective on how the advent of language might magnify our cognitive powers if we concentrate instead on why and how a *spoken* language of thought—an offspring of our natural, public language— might do some good work.

TALKING TO OURSELVES
········

> If the untrained infant's mind is to become an
> intelligent one, it must acquire both discipline
> and initiative.
>
> Alan Turing

There is no step more uplifting, more explosive, more momentous in the history of mind design than the invention of language. When *Homo sapiens* became the beneficiary of this invention, the species stepped into a slingshot that has launched it far beyond all other earthly species in the power to look ahead and reflect. What is true of the species is just as true of the individual. No transition is more astronomically enabling in the life of an individual person than "learning" to speak. I must put the word in scare-quotes, since we have come to realize (thanks to the work of linguists and psycholinguists) that human infants are genetically predesigned for language in many ways. As the father of modern linguistics, Noam Chomsky, often says (with excusable exaggeration), birds don't have to learn their feathers and babies don't have to learn their language. Much of the hard work of designing a language user (or a feather user) was accomplished eons ago and is provided to the infant in the form of innate talents and dispositions, readily adapted to local conditions of vocabulary and grammar. Children acquire language at breathtaking speed, picking up new words at an average rate of a dozen a day, for years on end, until they become adolescents, when the rate slows to a trickle. They master all but the finest points of their grammar before they enter school. In addition to all their linguistic interactions with their family members (and pets), babies and toddlers spend many hours vocalizing to themselves, first babbling, then indulging in marvelous mixtures of words and nonsense syllables richly endowed with different tones of voice—hortatory, soothing, explanatory, cajoling—and eventually evolving into elaborate self-commentary.

Children enjoy talking to themselves. What might this be doing to their minds? I cannot answer that question yet, but I have some speculative suggestions for further research. Consider what happens early in the linguistic life of any child. "Hot!" says Mother. "Don't touch the stove!" At this point, the child doesn't have to know what "hot" or "touch" or "stove" means—these words are *primarily* just sounds, auditory event-types that have a certain redolence, a certain familiarity, a certain echoing memorability to the child. They come to conjure up a situation-type—stove-approach-and-avoidance—which is not just a situation in which a specific prohibition is typically *heard* but also a situation in which a mimicking auditory rehearsal is encountered. Crudely simplifying, let's suppose that the child acquires the habit of saying to itself (aloud) "Hot!" "Don't touch!" without much of an idea what these words mean, voicing them merely as an associated part of the drill that goes with approaching and then avoiding the stove—and also as a sort of mantra, which might be uttered at any other time. After all, children are taken with the habit of rehearsing words they have just heard—rehearsing them in and out of context and building up recognition links and association paths between the auditory properties and concurrent sensory properties, internal states, and so forth.

That's a rough sketch of the sort of process that must go on. This process could have the effect of initiating a habit of what we might call *semi-understood self-commentary*. The child, prompted initially by some insistent auditory associations provoked by its parents' admonitions, acquires the habit of adding a sound track to its activities—"commenting" on them. The actual utterances would consist at the outset of large measures of "scribble"—nonsense talk composed of wordlike sounds—mixed with real words mouthed with much feeling but little or no appreciation of their meaning, and a few understood words. There would be mock exhortation, mock prohibition, mock praise, mock description, and all these would eventually mature into real exhortation, prohibition, praise, and description. But the habit of adding "labels" would thus be driven into place before the labels themselves were understood, or even partially understood.

I'm suggesting that it's such initially "stupid" practices—the mere mouthing of labels, in circumstances appropriate and inappropriate—that could soon turn into the habit of representing one's own states and activities to oneself in a new way. As the child lays down more associations between the auditory and articulatory processes on the one hand, and patterns of concurrent activity on the other, this would create nodes of saliency in memory. A word can become familiar even without being understood. And it is these anchors of familiarity that could give a label an independent identity within the system. Without such independence, labels are invisible. For a word to serve as a useful, manipulable label in the refinement of the resources of a brain, it must be a ready *enhancer* of sought-for associations that are already to some extent laid down in the system. Beyond that, words can be arbitrary, and their arbitrariness is actually part of what makes them distinctive: there is little risk of failing to notice the presence of the label; it doesn't just blend into its surroundings, like a dent in the corner of a shoebox. It wears the deliberateness of its creation on its sleeve.

The habit of semi-understood self-commentary could, I am suggesting, be the origin of the practice of deliberate labeling, in words (or scribble words or other private neologisms), which in turn could lead to a still more efficient practice: dropping all or most of the auditory and articulatory associations and just relying on the *rest* of the associations (and association-possibilities) to do the anchoring. The child, I suggest, can abandon out-loud mouthings and create private, unvoiced neologisms as labels for features of its own activities.

We can take a linguistic object as a *found object* (even if we have somehow blundered into making it ourselves rather than hearing it from someone else) and store it away for further consideration, off-line. Our ability to do this depends on our ability to re-identify or recognize such a label on different occasions, and this in turn depends on the label having some feature or features by which to remember it—some guise independent of its meaning. Once we have created labels and acquired the habit of attaching them to experienced circumstances, we have created a new class of objects that can themselves become the objects of all the pattern-recognition machinery, association-building machinery, and so forth. Like the scientists lingering retrospectively over an unhurried examination of the photographs they took in the heat of experimental battle, we can reflect on whatever patterns there are to be discerned in the various labeled exhibits we dredge out of memory.

As we improve, our labels become ever more refined, more perspicuous, ever better articulated, and the point is finally reached when we approximate the near-magical prowess we began with: the *mere contemplation* of a representation is sufficient to call to mind all the appropriate lessons. We have become *understanders* of the objects we have created. We might call these artifactual nodes in our memories, these pale shadows of articulated and heard words, *concepts*. A concept, then, is an internal label which may or may not include among its many associations the auditory and articulatory features of a word (public or private). But words, I am suggesting, are the prototypes or forebears of concepts. The first concepts one can manipulate, I am suggesting, are "voiced" concepts, and only concepts that can be manipulated can become objects of scrutiny for us.

Plato, in the *Theætetus*, compares human memory to a huge cage of birds:

SOCRATES: Now consider whether knowledge is a thing you can possess in that way without having it about you, like a man who has caught some wild birds—pigeons or what not—and keeps them in an aviary for them at home. In a sense, of course, we might say that he "has" them all the time inasmuch as he possesses them, mightn't we?

THEÆTETUS: Yes.

SOCRATES: But in another sense he "has" none of them, though he has got control of them, now that he has made them captive in an enclosure of his own; he can

> take and have hold of them whenever he likes by catching any bird he chooses, and let them go again; and it is open to him to do that as often as he pleases. (197c-d, Cornford translation)

The trick is: getting the right bird to come when you need it. How do we do it? By means of technology. We build elaborate systems of mnemonic association—pointers, labels, chutes and ladders, hooks and chains. We refine our resources by incessant rehearsal and tinkering, turning our brains (and all the associated peripheral gear we acquire) into a huge structured network of competences. No evidence yet unearthed shows that any other animal does anything like that.

....

CHAPTER 6

OUR MINDS AND OTHER MINDS

Once the child has learned the meaning of "why" and "because," he has become a fully paid-up member of the human race.

Elaine Morgan, *The Descent of the Child: Human Evolution from a New Perspective*

OUR CONSCIOUSNESS, THEIR MINDS
....

A mind looks less miraculous when one sees how it might have been put together out of parts, and how it still relies on those parts. A naked human mind—without paper and pencil, without speaking, comparing notes, making sketches—is first of all something we have never seen. Every human mind you've ever looked at—including most especially your own, which you look at "from the inside"— is a product not just of natural selection but of cultural redesign of enormous proportions. It's easy enough to see why a mind seems miraculous, when one has no sense of all the components and of how they got made. Each component has a long design history, sometimes billions of years long.

Before any creature could think, there were creatures with crude, unthinking intentionality—mere tracking and discriminating devices that had no inkling of what they were doing or why. But they worked well. These devices tracked things, reliably responding to their twists and turns, keeping on target for the most part, and seldom straying for long before returning to their task. Over much longer time spans, the *designs* of these devices could also be said to track something: not evasive mates, or prey, but something abstract— the free-floating rationales of their own functions. As circumstances changed, the designs of the devices changed in appropriate reponse to the new conditions, keeping their owners well equipped without burdening them with the reasons. These creatures hunted, but didn't think they were hunting, fled but didn't think they were fleeing. They had the *know-how* they needed. Know-how is a kind of wisdom, a kind of useful information, but it is not represented knowledge.

Then some creatures began to refine that part of the environment that was easiest to control, putting marks both inside and outside—off-loading problems into the world, and just into other parts of their brains. They began making and using representations, but they didn't know they were doing so. They didn't need to know. Should we call this sort of unwitting use of representations "thinking"? If so, then we would have to say that these creatures were thinking, but didn't know they were thinking! Unconscious thinking— those with a taste for "paradoxical" formulations might favor this way of speaking, but we could less misleadingly say that this was *intelligent but unthinking* behavior, because it was not just not reflective but also not reflectable-upon.

We human beings do many intelligent things unthinkingly. We brush our teeth, tie our shoes, drive our cars, and even answer questions without thinking. But most of these activities of ours are different, for we *can* think about them in ways that other creatures can't think about their unthinking but intelligent activities. Indeed, many of our unthinking activities, such as driving a car, could become unthinking only after passing through a long period of design development that was explicitly self-conscious. How is this accomplished? The improvements we install in our brains when we learn our languages permit us to review, recall, rehearse, redesign our own activities, turning our brains into echo chambers of sorts, in which otherwise evanescent processes can hang around and become objects in their own right. Those that persist the longest, acquiring influence as they persist, we call our conscious thoughts.

Mental contents become conscious not by entering some special chamber in the brain, not by being transduced into some privileged and mysterious medium, but by winning the competitions against other mental contents for domination in the control of behavior, and hence for achieving long-lasting effects—or as we misleadingly say, "entering into memory." And since we are talkers, and since talking to ourselves is one of our most influential activities, one of the most effective ways for a mental content to become influential is for it to get into position to drive the language-using parts of the controls.

A common reaction to this suggestion about human consciousness is frank bewilderment, expressed more or less as follows: "Suppose all these strange competitive processes are going on in my brain, and suppose that, as you say, the conscious processes are simply those that win the competitions. How does *that* make them conscious? What happens next to them that makes it true that *I* know about them? For after all, it is *my* consciousness, as I know it from the first-person point of view, that needs explaining!" Such questions betray a deep confusion, for they presuppose that what *you* are is something *else*, some Cartesian *res cogitans* in addition to all this brain-and-body activity. What you are, however, just *is* this organization of all the competitive activity between a host of competences that your body has developed. You "automatically" know about these things going on in your body, because if you didn't, it wouldn't be your body! (You could walk off with somebody else's gloves, mistakenly thinking they were your gloves, but you couldn't sign a contract with somebody else's hand, mistakenly thinking it was your hand, and you couldn't be overcome by somebody else's sadness or fear, mistakenly thinking it was your own.)

The acts and events you can tell us about, and the reasons for them, are yours because you made them—and because they made you. What you are is that agent whose life you can tell about. You can tell us, and you can tell yourself. The process of self-description begins in earliest childhood and includes a good deal of fantasy from the outset. (Think of Snoopy in the *Peanuts* cartoon, sitting on his doghouse and thinking, "Here's the World War I ace, flying into battle.") It continues through life. (Think of the café waiter in Jean-Paul Sartre's discussion of "bad faith" in *Being and Nothingness*, who is all wrapped up in learning how to live up to his self-description as a waiter.) It is what *we* do. It is what *we* are.

Are other minds really so different from human minds? As a simple experiment, I would like you to imagine something that I daresay you've never imagined before. Please imagine, in some detail, a man in a white lab coat climbing hand over hand up a rope while holding a red plastic bucket in his teeth. An easy mental task for you. Could a chimpanzee perform the same mental task? I wonder. I chose the elements—man, rope, climbing, bucket, teeth—as familiar objects in the perceptual and behavioral world of a laboratory chimp. I'm sure that such a chimp can not only perceive such things but see them *as* a man, a rope, a bucket, and so forth. In some minimal sense, then, I grant that the chimp has a *concept* of a man, a rope, a bucket (but does not have concepts, presumably, of a lobster, or a limerick, or a lawyer). My question is, What can a chimp do with its concepts? Back during World War I, the German psychologist Wolfgang Köhler did some famous experiments with chimps to see what sort of problems they could solve by thinking: Could a chimp figure out how to stack some boxes in its cage to get at some bananas hanging from the ceiling which were too high to for it to reach? Alternatively, could it figure out how to fasten two sticks together into one long enough to knock the food down? The popular lore holds that Köhler's chimps could indeed figure out these solutions, but in fact the animals were quite unimpressive in action; some solved the problems only after many, many trials, and others never saw the light. Later studies, including some current ones that are much more subtle, still fail to settle these apparently simple questions about what a chimp can think when provided with all the clues. But let's suppose for the moment that Köhler's experiments did answer the question they are commonly reputed to have answered: that a chimp can indeed discover the solution to a simple problem of this sort, provided that the elements of the solution are visible and ready to hand—available for trial-and-error manipulation.

My question is different: Can a chimpanzee *call to mind* the elements of a solution when these elements are not present to provide the chimp with visible reminders of themselves? The exercise you engaged in was provoked by a verbal suggestion from me. I am sure that you can just as readily make suggestions to yourself, and then take your own suggestions, thereby framing mental imagery of considerable novelty. (That's one of the things *we* know about ourselves—that we all enjoy engaging in elaborate exercises of imagination carefully tailored to meet our interests of the moment.)

The account I've sketched in previous chapters of how non-human minds work implies that chimps should be incapable of such activities. They might somehow happen to put together the relevant concepts (their sort of concepts) by accident, and then have their attention drawn to any serendipitously interesting results, but even that, I suspect, is beyond the limits of their resources' movability or manipulability.

These questions about the minds of chimps are rather simple, but nobody knows the answers—yet. The answers are not impossible to acquire, but devising suitable experiments is not easy. Notice that these questions are not the sort that can be addressed by looking at the relative size of the animal's brain, or even gauging its brute cognitive capacity (of memory, of discriminatory prowess). Surely there is plenty of machinery in a chimp's brain to store all the information needed as raw material for such a task; the question is whether the machinery is organized in such a way as to permit this sort of exploitation. (You have a big aviary, with plenty of birds; can you get them to fly in formation?) What makes a mind powerful—indeed, what makes a mind conscious—is not what it is made of, or how big it is, but what it can do. Can it concentrate? Can it be distracted? Can it recall earlier events? Can it keep track of several different things at once? Which features of its own current activities can it notice or monitor?

When such questions as these are answered, we will know everything we need to know about those minds in order to answer the morally important questions. These answers will capture everything we want to know about the concept of consciousness, *except* the idea of whether, as one author has recently said, "the mental lights would be out" in such a creature. But that's just a bad idea—in spite of its popularity. Not only has it never been defined or even clarified by any of its champions; there is no work for such a clarification or definition to do. For suppose that we have indeed answered all the other questions about the mind of some creature, and now some philosophers claim that we still don't know the answer to that all-important question, Is the mental light on—yes or no? Why would either answer be important? We are owed an answer to *this* question, before we need to take their question seriously.

Does a dog have a concept of *cat*? Yes *and* no. No matter how close a dog's "concept" of cat is to yours extensionally (you and the dog discriminate the same sets of entities as cats and noncats), it differs radically in one way: the dog cannot consider its concept. It cannot ask itself whether it knows what cats are; it cannot wonder whether cats are animals; it cannot attempt to distinguish the essence of cat (by its lights) from the mere accidents. Concepts are not things in the dog's world in the way that cats are. Concepts *are* things in our world, because we have language. A polar bear is competent vis-à-vis snow in many ways that a lion is not, so in one sense a polar bear has a concept that the lion lacks—a concept of snow. But no languageless mammal can have the concept of snow in the way we can, because a languageless mammal has no way of considering snow "in general" or "in itself." This is not for the trivial reason that it doesn't have a (natural-language) *word* for snow but because without a natural language it has no talent for wresting concepts from their interwoven connectionist nests and manipulating them. We can speak of the polar bear's implicit or procedural knowledge of snow (the polar bear's *snow-how*), and we can even investigate, empirically, the extension of the polar bear's embedded snow-concept, but then bear in mind that this is not a wieldable concept for the polar bear.

"It may not be able to talk, but surely it thinks!"—one of the main aims of this book has been to shake your confidence in this familiar reaction. Perhaps the biggest obstacle in our attempts to get clear about the mental competences of nonhuman animals is our almost irresistible habit of imagining that they accompany their clever activities with a stream of reflective consciousness *something* like our own. It is not that we now *know* that they don't do any such thing; it is rather that in these early days of our investigations we must not *assume* that they do. Both the philosophical and scientific thinking about this issue has been heavily influenced by the philosopher Thomas Nagel's classic 1974 paper, "What Is It Like to Be a Bat?" The title itself sets us off on the wrong foot, inviting us to ignore all the different ways in which bats (and other animals) might accomplish their cunning feats without its "being like" anything for them. We create a putatively impenetrable mystery for ourselves if we presume without further ado that Nagel's question makes sense, and that we know what we are asking.

What is it like for a bird to build a nest? The question invites you to imagine how you would build a nest and then to try to imagine the details of the comparison. But since nest building is not something you habitually do, you should first remind yourself of what it's like for you to do something familiar. Well, what is it like for you to tie your shoelaces? Sometimes you pay attention; sometimes it gets done by your fingers without any notice at all, while you think of other things. So maybe, you may think, the bird is daydreaming or plotting tomorrow's activities while it executes its constructive moves. Maybe, but in fact the evidence to date strongly suggests that the bird is not equipped to do any such thing. Indeed, the contrast you note between paying attention and doing the task while your mind was otherwise occupied probably has no counterpart at all in the case of the bird. The fact that *you* couldn't build a nest without thinking carefully and reflectively about what you were doing and why is not at all a good reason for assuming that when the bird builds its nest, it must think its birdish thoughts about what it is doing (at least for its first nest, before it has mastered the task). The more we learn about how brains can engage in processes that accomplish clever deeds for their nonhuman owners, the less these processes look like the thoughts we had dimly imagined to be doing the work. That doesn't mean that *our* thoughts are not processes occurring in our brains, or that our thoughts are not playing the critical roles in governing our behavior that we normally assume they are. Presumably some of the processes in our own human brains will eventually be discernible as the thoughts we know so intimately, but it remains to be seen whether the mental *competences* of any other species depend on their having mental *lives* the way we do.

PAIN AND SUFFERING: WHAT MATTERS
········

> There is always a well-known solution to every
> human problem—neat, plausible, and wrong.
>   H. L. Mencken, *Prejudices* (second series)

It would be reassuring if we had come to the end of our story and could say something along the lines of "And so we see that it follows from our discoveries that insects and fish and reptiles aren't sentient after all—they are mere automata—but amphibians, birds, and mammals are sentient or conscious just like us! And, for the record, a human fetus becomes sentient at between fifteen and sixteen weeks." Such a neat, plausible solution to some of our human problems of moral decision making would be a great relief, but no such story can be told yet, and there is no reason to believe that such a story will unfold later. It is unlikely that we have entirely overlooked a feature of mentality that would make all the difference to morality, and the features we have examined seem to make their appearance not just gradually but in an unsynchronized, inconsistent, and patchy fashion, both in evolutionary history and in the development of individual organisms. It is *possible*, of course, that further research will reveal a heretofore undetectable system of similarities and differences which will properly impress us, and we will then be able to see, for the first time, where nature has drawn the line, and why. This is not a possibility on which to lean, however, if we can't even imagine what such a discovery might be, or why it would strike us as morally relevant. (We might just as well imagine that one fine day the clouds will part and God will tell us, directly, which creatures to include and which to exclude from the charmed circle.)

In our survey of kinds of minds (and protominds) there does not seem to be any clear threshold or critical mass— until we arrive at the sort of consciousness that we language-using human beings enjoy. That variety of mind is unique, and orders of magnitude more powerful than any other variety of mind, but we probably don't want to rest too much moral weight on it. We might well think that the capacity for suffering counts for more, in any moral calculations, than the capacity for abstruse and sophisticated reasoning about the future (and everything else under the sun). What, then, is the relationship between pain, suffering, and consciousness?

While the distinction between pain and suffering is, like most everyday, nonscientific distinctions, somewhat blurred at the edges, it is nevertheless a valuable and intuitively satisfying mark or measure of moral importance. The phenomenon of pain is neither homogeneous across species, nor simple. We can see this in ourselves, by noting how unobvious the answers are to some simple questions. Are the stimuli from our pain receptors—stimuli that prevent us from allowing our limbs to assume awkward, joint-damaging positions while we sleep—experienced as pains? Or might they be

properly called unconscious pains? Do they have moral significance, in any case? We might call such body-protecting
states of the nervous system "sentient" states, without
thereby implying that they were the experiences of any self,
any ego, any subject. For such states to matter—whether or
not we call them pains, or conscious states, or experiences—
there must be an enduring subject *to whom* they matter
because they are a source of suffering.

Consider the widely reported phenomenon of *dissociation* in the presence of great pain or fear. When young children are abused, they typically hit upon a desperate but
effective stratagem: they "leave." They somehow declare to
themselves that it is not they who are suffering the pain.
There seem to be two main varieties of dissociators: those
who simply reject the pain as theirs and then witness it from
afar, as it were; and those who split at least momentarily into
something like multiple personalities ("I" am not undergoing this pain, *"she"* is). My not entirely facetious hypothesis
about this is that these two varieties of children differ in
their tacit endorsement of a philosophical doctrine: Every
experience must be the experience of some subject. Those
children who reject the principle see nothing wrong with
simply disowning the pain, leaving it subjectless to wander
around hurting nobody in particular. Those who embrace
the principle have to invent an alter to be the subject—"anybody but *me!*"

Whether or not any such interpretation of the phenomenon of dissociation can be sustained, most psychiatrists
agree that it does work, to some degree. That is, whatever
this psychological stunt of dissociation consists in, it is gen-
uinely analgesic—or, more precisely, whether or not it
diminishes the *pain*, it definitely *obtunds suffering*. So we
have a modest result of sorts: the difference, whatever it is,
between a nondissociated child and a dissociated child is a
difference that markedly affects the existence or amount of

suffering. (I hasten to add that nothing I have said implies that when children dissociate they in any way mitigate the atrocity of the vile behavior of their abusers; they do, however, dramatically diminish the awfulness of the effects themselves—though such children may pay a severe price later in life in dealing with the aftereffects of their dissociation.)

A dissociated child does not suffer as much as a nondissociated child. But now what should we say about creatures that are *naturally* dissociated—that never achieve, or even attempt to achieve, the sort of complex internal organization that is standard in a normal child and disrupted in a dissociated child? An invited conclusion would be: such a creature is constitutionally incapable of undergoing the *sort* or *amount* of suffering that a normal human can undergo. But if all nonhuman species are in such a relatively disorganized state, we have grounds for the hypothesis that nonhuman animals may indeed feel pain but cannot suffer the way we can.

How convenient! Animal lovers can be expected to respond to this suggestion with righteous indignation and deep suspicion. Since it does indeed promise to allay many of our misgivings about common human practices, absolving our hunters and farmers and experimenters of at least some of the burden of guilt that others would place on their shoulders, we should be particularly cautious and even-handed in considering the grounds for it. We should be on the lookout for sources of illusion—on both sides of this stormy issue. The suggestion that nonhuman animals are not susceptible to human levels of suffering typically provokes a flood of heart-wrenching stories—mostly about dogs. Why do dogs predominate? Could it be that dogs make the best counterexamples because dogs actually do have a greater capacity for suffering than other mammals? It could be, and the evolutionary perspective we have been pursuing can explain why.

Dogs, and only dogs among domesticated species,

respond strongly to the enormous volume of what we might call "humanizing" behavior aimed at them by their owners. We talk to our dogs, commiserate with our dogs, and in general treat them as much like a human companion as we can—and we delight in their familiar and positive response to this friendliness. We may try it with cats, but it seldom seems to take. This is not surprising, in retrospect; domestic dogs are the descendants of social mammals, accustomed over millions of years to living in cooperative, highly interactive groups, while domestic cats spring from asocial lineages. Moreover, domestic dogs are importantly unlike their cousins, the wolves and foxes and coyotes, in their responsiveness to human affection. There is no mystery about why this should be so. Domestic dogs have been selected for just these differences for hundreds of thousands of generations. In *The Origin of Species*, Charles Darwin pointed out that whereas deliberate human intervention in the reproduction of domesticated species has worked for several thousand years to breed faster horses, woollier sheep, beefier cattle, and so forth, a more subtle but still powerful force has been at work for a much longer time shaping our domesticated species. He called it unconscious selection. Our ancestors engaged in selective breeding, but they didn't think they were doing so. This unwitting favoritism, over the eons, has made our dogs more and more like us in ways that appeal to us. Among other traits we have unconsciously selected for, I suggest, is susceptibility to human socializing, which has, in dogs, many of the organizing effects that human socializing also has on human infants. By treating them as if they were human, we actually succeed in making them more human than they otherwise would be. They begin to develop the very organizational features that are otherwise the sole province of socialized human beings. In short, if human consciousness—the sort of consciousness that is a necessary condition for serious suffering—is, as I have maintained, a radical restructuring of the virtual architecture of the human brain, then it should follow that the only animals that would be capable of anything remotely like that form of consciousness would be animals that could also have imposed on them, by culture, that virtual machine. Dogs are clearly closest to meeting this condition.

What about pain? When I step on your toe, causing a brief but definite (and definitely conscious) pain, I do you scant harm—typically none at all. The pain, though intense, is too brief to matter, and I have done no long-term damage to your foot. The idea that you "suffer" for a second or two is a risible misapplication of that important notion, and even when we grant that my causing you a few seconds of pain may irritate you for a few seconds or even minutes more—especially if you think I did it deliberately—the pain itself, as a brief, negatively-signed experience, is of vanishing moral significance. (If in stepping on your toe I have interrupted your singing of the aria, thereby ruining your operatic career, that is quite another matter.)

Many discussions seem to assume tacitly (1) that suffering and pain are the same thing, on a different scale; (2) that all pain is "experienced pain"; and (3) that the "amount of suffering" is to be calculated ("in principle") just by adding up all the pains (the awfulness of each of which is determined by duration-times-intensity). These assumptions, looked at dispassionately in the cold light of day (a difficult feat for some partisans), are ludicrous. A little exercise may help: Suppose, thanks to some "miracle of modern medicine," you could detach all your pain and suffering from the contexts in which it occurred, postponing it all, say, to the end of the year, when it could be endured in one horrible week of unremitting agony, a sort of negative vacation, or—if the formula of assumption (3) is to be taken seriously—trading off duration for intensity, so that a year's misery could be packed into one excruciating lump-sum jolt lasting, say, five minutes. A whole year without so much as a mild annoyance or headache in exchange for a brief and entirely reversible descent into hell-without-anesthesia—would you accept such a bargain? I certainly would, if I thought it made sense. (We are assuming, of course, that this horrible episode would not kill me or render me insane in the aftermath—though I'd be quite happy to be insane during the jolt itself!) In fact, I'd gladly take the bargain even if it meant "doubling" or "quadrupling" the total amount of suffering, just as long as it would be all over in five minutes and leave no lasting debilities. I expect anybody would be happy to make such a deal, but it doesn't really make sense. (It would imply, for instance, that the benefactor who provided such a service gratis to all would, *ex hypothesi*, double or quadruple the world's suffering—and the world would love him for it.)

What's wrong with this scenario is, of course, that you can't detach pain and suffering from their contexts in the imagined way. The anticipation and aftermath, and the recognition of the implications for one's life plans and prospects, cannot be set aside as the "merely cognitive" accompaniments of the suffering. What is awful about losing your job, or your leg, or your reputation, or your loved one is not the suffering this event *causes* in you, but the suffering this event *is*. If we are concerned to discover and ameliorate unacknowledged instances of suffering in the world, we need to study creatures' lives, not their brains. What happens in their brains is of course highly relevant as a rich source of evidence about what they are doing and how they do it, but what they are doing is in the end just as visible—to a trained observer—as the activities of plants, mountain streams, or internal combustion engines. If we fail to find suffering in the lives we can see (studying them diligently, using all the methods of science), we can rest assured that there is no invisible suffering somewhere in their brains. If we find suffering, we will recognize it without difficulty. It is all too familiar.

This book began with a host of questions, and—since this is a book by a philosopher—it ends not with the answers, but, I hope, with better versions of the questions themselves. At least we can see some paths to pursue, and some traps to avoid, in our ongoing exploration of the different kinds of minds.

It might seem that there would be little point in your reading the books that have influenced me the most in writing this book, since if I have done my work well, I have already extracted the best bits, saving you the time and trouble. That's true of some of them, perhaps, but not the books I list here. These are books that I particularly want my readers to read, if they haven't already read them, and read again if they have. I have learned a lot from them—but not enough! I am acutely aware, in fact, that there is much more for me (and everybody else) to find in these books, and in some ways this book is meant as an inducement and guide.

First, I submit two famous and influential but often misunderstood books by philosophers: *The Concept of Mind* (1949), by Gilbert Ryle, and *Philosophical Investigations* (1958), by Ludwig Wittgenstein. Both Ryle and Wittgenstein were quite hostile to the idea of a scientific investigation of the mind, and the standard wisdom in the "cognitive revolution" is that we have seen through and beyond their ruthlessly unscientific analyses of the mental. Not true. One has to tolerate their often frustrating misperception of good scientific questions, and their almost total ignorance of biology and brain science, but they still managed to make deep and important observations that most of us are only now getting into position to appreciate. Ryle's account of "knowing how" (as distinct from "knowing that") has long attracted the attention and approval of cognitive scientists, but his notorious claims that thinking could happen out in the public world and didn't have to go on in some private thinking place have seemed perverse and ill motivated to most readers. Some of them no doubt were, but it is surprising to see how much of Ryle's thought shines when new light is directed upon it. Wittgenstein, meanwhile, has suffered the admiration of a horde of misunderstanders who share his antipathy to science but not his vision. They can be safely ignored; go to the original, and read it through the lens I have tried to provide. A similarly placed figure is the psychologist James J. Gibson, whose amazingly original book *The Senses Considered as Perceptual Systems* (1968) has been a lightning rod for misdirected attacks from cognitive scientists and a holy text for an all-too-devoted cabal of radical Gibsonians. Read it; save them for later.

Valentino Braitenberg's *Vehicles: Experiments in Synthetic Psychology* (1984) has inspired a generation of roboticists and other cognitive scientists and is, simply, a classic. It will change the way you think about the mind, if my book has not already accomplished that transformation. Another philosopher who has drunk deeply at Braitenberg's well is Dan Lloyd, and his 1989 book, *Simple Minds*, covers much of the ground that this book does, with somewhat different emphases but, I think, no major disagreements. Dan Lloyd was my informal student and junior colleague at Tufts when he was working on his book. I simply cannot tell what he has taught me and I him; there is a lot to learn from his book in any case. I could say the same about some other colleagues of mine at the Center at Tufts, Kathleen Akins, Nicholas Humphrey, and Evan Thompson. It was Akins who first showed me, back in the mid–1980s, why and how we must escape old-fashioned epistemology and ontology when thinking about animal minds. See, for instance, her essays "Science and our Inner Lives: Birds of Prey, Beasts, and the Common (Featherless) Biped" and "What Is It Like to Be Boring and Myopic?" Nicholas Humphrey came to work with me for several years in 1987, but I still haven't come to terms with all the ideas in his *A History of the Mind* (1992), in spite of many hours of discussion. While Evan Thompson was at the Center, he was finishing his coauthored book, with Francisco Varela and Eleanor Rosch, *The Embodied Mind* (1990), and the influences of that book in this book can be readily seen,

I am sure. More recently, Antonio Damasio's *Descartes' Error: Emotion, Reason, and the Human Brain* (1994) consolidates and advances some of the themes in these works, in addition to opening up new ground of its own.

For a deeper understanding of the role of evolution in designing the minds of all creatures, you should read all of Richard Dawkins' books, beginning with *The Selfish Gene*. Robert Trivers' *Social Evolution* is an excellent introduction to the fine points of sociobiology. The new field of evolutionary psychology is well represented in an anthology edited by Jerome Barkow, Leda Cosmides, and John Tooby, *The Adapted Mind: Evolutionary Psychology and the Generation of Culture* (1992), and for an eye-opening rethinking of child psychology and child biology, read Elaine Morgan, *The Descent of the Child: Human Evolution from a New Perspective* (1995).

On another front, the cognitive ethologists have filled out philosophers' (and psychologists') fantasies about the mental lives and powers of nonhuman animals with a flood of fascinating experimental and observational work. Donald Griffin is the father of the field. His books *The Question of Animal Awareness* (1976), *Animal Thinking* (1984), and *Animal Minds* (1992) but even more important, his pioneering investigations of bats' echolocation, opened the minds of many to the possibilities in this field. An exemplary study is Dorothy Cheney and Robert Seyfarth's work with vervet monkeys, *How Monkeys See the World* (1990). Andrew Whiten and Richard Byrne's anthology, *Machiavellian Intelligence* (1988), and Carolyn Ristau's anthology, *Cognitive Ethology* (1991), provide both classic texts and astringent analyses of the problems; and a beautifully illustrated book by James and Carol Gould, *The Animal Mind* (1994), should flavor the theoretical imaginations of everybody who thinks about animal minds. For the very latest on animal thinking and communication, see Marc Hauser's new book, *The Evolution of Communication*, and Derek Bickerton's *Language and Human Behavior*. Patrick Bateson's 1991 essay, "Assessment of Pain in Animals," is a valuable overview of what is known and still unknown about animal pain and suffering.

In chapter 4, I passed swiftly (but reluctantly so) over a large and fascinating literature on higher-order intentionality—children and animals as "natural psychologists." I could get away with this swiftness, I decided, because the topic has received so much good attention elsewhere recently. Two excellent books—among many—that explain both the details and why it is important are Janet Astington's *The Child's Discovery of the Mind* (1993) and Simon Baron-Cohen's *Mindblindness* (1995).

I also skimped on the important topic of ABC learning and its most promising current models. For the details (and some nontrivial differences of philosophical opinion well worth considering) see Andy Clark, *Associative Engines: Connectionism, Concepts and Representational Change* (1993), and Paul Churchland, *The Engine of Reason, the Seat of the Soul* (1995). Those who want to get even more serious about the details (which I recommend) can start with Patricia Churchland and Terence Sejnowski, *The Computational Brain* (1992). Consider these books an important reality check on some of my more impressionistic and enthusiastic speculations. Two more philosophers whose work should be consulted by anyone who wants to evaluate the claims I have advanced here by triangulating them with some related but quite orthogonal visions are Gareth Evans, *The Varieties of Reference* (1982), and Ruth Garrett Millikan, *Language Thought and Other Biological Categories* (1984) and *White Queen Psychology and Other Essays for Alice* (1993).

The discussion of making things to think with in chapters 5 and 6 was inspired not just by Richard Gregory's *Mind in Science* (1981) and Andy Clark and Annette Karmiloff-Smith's 1993 paper, but also by Karmiloff-Smith's book *Beyond Modularity* (1992), and by several earlier books that have been fruitfully rattling around in my brain for years: Julian Jaynes' *The Origins of Consciousness in the Breakdown of the Bicameral Mind* (1976), George Lakoff and Mark Johnson's *Metaphors We Live By* (1980), Philip Johnson-Laird's *Mental Models* (1983), and Marvin Minsky's *The Society of Mind* (1985). A new book that presents the first actual models of some of these quintessentially human activities is Douglas Hofstadter's *Fluid Concepts and Creative Analogies: Computer Models of the Fundamental Mechanisms of Thought* (1995).

My 1991 book *Consciousness Explained* was primarily about human consciousness, saying little about the minds of other animals except by implication. Since some readers who tried to work out those implications arrived at positions they found dubious or even alarming, I realized that I had to clarify my theory of consciousness, extending it explicitly to other species. *Kinds of Minds* is one result; another is "Animal Consciousness: What Matters and Why," my contribution to the conference "In the Company of Animals," held at the New School for Social Research, in New York City, April 1995. The evolutionary underpinnings of my theory of consciousness have also met with skepticism, which I have addressed in my 1995 book, *Darwin's Dangerous Idea.* Many of the claims I advance in *Kinds of Minds* are drawn from, or are elaborated upon in, other articles of mine listed in the bibliography.

Akins, Kathleen, "Science and Our Inner Lives: Birds of Prey, Beasts, and the Common (Featherless) Biped," in Marc Bekoff and Dale Jamieson, eds., *Interpretation and Explanation in the Study of Animal Behavior*, Vol. 1 (Boulder, Colo.: Westview, 1990), 414–427.

———, "What Is It Like to Be Boring and Myopic?" in Dahlbom, ed., *Dennett and His Critics*.

Astington, Janet, *The Child's Discovery of the Mind* (Cambridge: Harvard University Press, 1993).

Balda, Russell P., and R. J. Turek, "Memory in Birds," in Herbert L. Roitblat, Thomas G. Bever, and Herbert S. Terrace, eds., *Animal Cognition* (Hillsdale, N.J.: Erlbaum, 1984), 513–532.

———, Alan C. Kamil, and Kristie Grim, "Revisits to Emptied Cache Sites by Clark's Nutcrackers (*Nucifraga columbiana*)," *Animal Behavior* 34 (1986), 1289–1298.

Barkow, Jerome, Leda Cosmides, and John Tooby, *The Adapted Mind: Evolutionary Psychology and the Generation of Culture* (Oxford: Oxford University Press, 1992).

Baron-Cohen, Simon, *Mindblindness: An Essay on Autism and Theory of Mind* (Cambridge: MIT Press/A Bradford Book, 1995).

Bateson, Patrick, "Assessment of Pain in Animals," *Animal Behavior* 42 (1991), 827–839.

Bickerton, Derek, *Language and Human Behavior* (Seattle: University of Washington Press, 1995).

Braitenberg, Valentino, *Vehicles: Experiments in Synthetic Psychology* (Cambridge, MIT Press/A Bradford Book, 1984).

Cheney, Dorothy, and Robert Seyfarth, *How Monkeys See the World* (Chicago: University of Chicago Press, 1990).

Churchland, Patricia, and Terence Sejnowski, *The Computational Brain* (Cambridge: MIT Press/A Bradford Book, 1992).

Churchland, Paul, *Scientific Realism and the Plasticity of Mind* (Cambridge, U.K.: Cambridge University Press, 1979).

———, *The Engine of Reason, the Seat of the Soul* (Cambridge: MIT Press/A Bradford Book, 1995).

Clark, Andy, *Associative Engines: Connectionism, Concepts and Representational Change* (Cambridge: MIT Press/A Bradford Book, 1993).

———, and Annette Karmiloff-Smith, "The Cognizer's Innards: A Psychological and Philosophical Perspective on the Development of Thought," *Mind and Language* 8 (1993), 487–519.

Dahlbom, Bo, ed., *Dennett and His Critics: Demystifying Mind* (Oxford: Blackwell, 1993).

Damasio, Antonio, *Descartes' Error: Emotion, Reason, and the Human Brain* (New York: Grosset/Putnam, 1994).

Darwin, Charles, *The Origin of Species* (London: Murray, 1859).

Dawkins, Richard, *The Selfish Gene* (Oxford: Oxford University Press, 1976; revised edition, 1989).

———, and John R. Krebs, "Animal Signals: Information or Manipulation?" in John R. Krebs and Nicholas B. Davies, eds., *Behavioural Ecology*, 2d ed. (Sunderland, Mass.: Sinauer Associates, 1978), 282–309.

Dennett, Daniel, "Brain Writing and Mind Reading," in K. Gunderson, ed., *Language, Mind and Knowledge, Minnesota Studies in the Philosophy of Science,* Vol. 7 (Minneapolis: University ofMinnesota Press, 1975). Reprinted in Dennett, *Brainstorms* and later with a postscript in D. Rosenthal, ed., *The Nature of Mind* (Oxford: Oxford University Press, 1991).

———, "Conditions of Personhood," in Amelie Rorty, ed., *The Identities of Persons* (Berkeley: University of California Press, 1976). Reprinted in Dennett, *Brainstorms.*

———, *Brainstorms* (Cambridge: MIT Press/A Bradford Book, 1978).

———, "Where Am I?" in Dennett, *Brainstorms*.

———, "Beyond Belief," in Andrew Woodfield, ed., *Thought and Object* (Oxford: Oxford University Press, 1982). Reprinted in Dennett, *The Intentional Stance*.

———, "Intentional Systems in Cognitive Ethology: The 'Panglossian Paradigm' Defended," *Behavioral and Brain Sciences* 6 (1983), 343–390.

———, *The Intentional Stance* (Cambridge: MIT Press/A Bradford Book, 1987).

———, *Consciousness Explained* (Boston: Little, Brown, 1991).

———, "Learning and Labeling" (commentary on Clark and Karmiloff-Smith), *Mind and Language* 8 (1993), 540–548.

———, "The Message Is: There Is No Medium" (reply to Jackson, Rosenthal, Shoemaker, and Tye), *Philosophy & Phenomenological Research*, December 1993, 889–931.

———, "Back from the Drawing Board" (reply to critics), in Dahlbom, ed., *Dennett and His Critics*.

———, *Darwin's Dangerous Idea* (New York: Simon & Schuster, 1995).

———, "Get Real" (reply to critics), in *Philosophical Topics*, 22 (1995), 505–568.

———, "Animal Consciousness: What Matters and Why," in *Social Research*, 62 (1995), 691–710.

———, forthcoming: "Consciousness: More like Fame than Television," for volume from the conference "Interfaces Brain-Computer," Christa Maar, Ernst Pöppel, and Thomas Christaller, eds., to be published by Rowohlt.

———, forthcoming: "Do Animals Have Beliefs?" in Herbert L. Roitblat, ed., *Comparative Approaches to Cognitive Sciences*, MIT Press.

Eigen, Manfred, *Steps Towards Life* (Oxford: Oxford University Press, 1992).

Evans, Gareth, *The Varieties of Reference* (Oxford: Clarendon Press, 1982).

Gaussier, Philippe, and Zrehen, S., A Constructivist Approach for Autonomous Agents," in Adia Magnenat Thalmann and Daniel Thalmann, eds., *Artificial Life and Virtual Reality* (London: Wiley, 1994).

———, "Avoiding the World Model Trap: An Acting Robot

Does Not Need to Be So Smart," *Robotics and Computer-Integrated Manufacturing* 11 (1994), 279–286.

Gibson, James J., *The Senses Considered as Perceptual Systems* (London: Allen & Unwin, 1968).

Gould, James, and Carol Gould, *The Animal Mind* (New York: HPHLP, Scientific American Library, 1994).

Gregory, Richard L., *Mind in Science: A History of Explanations in Psychology* (Cambridge, U.K.: Cambridge University Press, 1981).

Griffin, Donald, *The Question of Animal Awareness* (New York: Rockefeller University Press, 1976).

———, *Animal Thinking* (Cambridge: Harvard University Press, 1984).

———, *Animal Minds* (Chicago: University of Chicago Press, 1992).

Hasson, O., "Pursuit-Deterrent Signals: Communication between Predator and Prey," *Trends in Ecology and Evolution* 6 (1991), 325–329.

Hebb, Donald, *The Organization of Behavior: A Neuropsychological Theory* (New York: Wiley, 1949).

Hofstadter, Douglas R., *Fluid Concepts and Creative Analogies: Computer Models of the Fundamental Mechanisms of Thought* (New York: Basic Books, 1995).

Holley, Tony, "No Hide, No Seek," *Natural History* 7 (1994), 42–45.

Humphrey, Nicholas, "Nature's Psychologists," *New Scientist* 29 (June 1978), 900–904. Reprinted in *Consciousness Regained* (Oxford: Oxford University Press, 1983).

———, *A History of the Mind* (London: Chatto & Windus, 1992).

Israel, David, John Perry, and Syun Tutiya, "Executions, Motivations and Accomplishments," *Philosophical Review* 102 (1993), 515–540.

Jaynes, Julian, *The Origins of Consciousness in the Breakdown of the Bicameral Mind* (Boston: Houghton Mifflin, 1976).

Johnson-Laird, Philip N., *Mental Models* (Cambridge, U.K.: Cambridge University Press, 1983).

Kamil, Alan C., Russell P. Balda, Deborah J. Olson, and Sally Good, "Returns to Emptied Cache Sites by Clark's Nutcrackers,

Nucifraga columbiana: A Puzzle Revisited," *Animal Behavior* 45 (1993), 241–252.

Karmiloff-Smith, Annette, *Beyond Modularity: A Developmental Perspective on Cognitive Science* (Cambridge: MIT Press/A Bradford Book, 1992).

Lakoff, George, and Mark Johnson, *Metaphors We Live By* (Chicago: University of Chicago Press, 1980).

Lloyd, Dan, *Simple Minds* (Cambridge: MIT Press/A Bradford Book, 1989).

McFarland, David, 1989, "Goals, No-Goals and Own Goals," in Alan Montefiore and Denis Noble, eds., *Goals, No-Goals and Own Goals: A Debate on Goal-Directed and Intentional Behaviour* (London: Unwin Hyman, 1989), 39–57.

Menzel, Emil W., Jr., 1971, "Communication about the Environment in a Group of Young Chimpanzees," *Folia Primatologia* 15 (1971), 220–232.

———, "A Group of Young Chimpanzees in a One-Acre Field," in A. M. Schreier and F. Stolnitz, eds., *Behavior of Nonhuman Primates*, Vol. 5 (New York: Academic Press, 1974), 83–153. Reprinted in Ristau, *Cognitive Ethology*.

Millikan, Ruth Garrett, *Language, Thought, and Other Biological Categories* (Cambridge: MIT Press/A Bradford Book, 1984).

———, *White Queen Psychology and Other Essays for Alice* (Cambridge: MIT Press/A Bradford Book, 1993).

———, "A Common Structure for Concepts of Individuals, Stuffs, and Basic Kin: More Mama, More Milk, and More Mouse," *Behavioral and Brain Sciences*, forthcoming.

Minsky, Marvin, *The Society of Mind* (New York: Simon & Schuster, 1985).

Morgan, Elaine, *The Descent of the Child: Human Evolution from a New Perspective* (Oxford: Oxford University Press, 1995).

Nagel, Thomas, "What Is It Like to Be a Bat?" *Philosophical Review* 83 (1974), 435–450.

Nietzsche, Friedrich, *Thus Spake Zarathustra*, Walter Kaufmann, trans. (New York: Viking, 1954).

Ristau, Carolyn, ed., *Cognitive Ethology* (Hillsdale, N.J.: Erlbaum, 1991).

————, "Aspects of the Cognitive Ethology of an Injury-Feigning Bird, the Piping Plover," in Ristau, ed., *Cognitive Ethology*, 91–126.

Ryle, Gilbert, *The Concept of Mind* (London: Hutchinson, 1949).

Sartre, Jean Paul, *Being and Nothingness* (*L'Etre et le Néant*), 1943, Hazel Barnes, trans. (New York: Philosophical Library, 1956; paperback ed., 1966).

Searle, John, "Minds, Brains and Programs," *Behavioral and Brain Sciences* 3 (1980), 417–458.

Skinner, B. F., *Science and Human Behavior* (New York: Macmillan, 1953).

————, "Behaviorism at Fifty," in T. W. Wann, ed., *Behaviorism and Phenomenology* (Chicago: University of Chicago Press, 1964), 79–108.

Sontag, Susan, *On Photography* (New York: Farrar, Straus & Giroux, 1977).

Thomas, Elizabeth Marshall, *The Hidden Life of Dogs* (Boston: Houghton Mifflin, 1993).

Trivers, Robert, *Social Evolution* (Menlo Park, Calif.: Benjamin Cummings, 1985).

Varela, Francisco J., Evan Thompson, and Eleanor Rosch, *The Embodied Mind: Cognitive Science and Human Experience* (Cambridge: MIT Press/A Bradford Book, 1991).

Whiten, Andrew, "Grades of Mind Reading," in Charlie Lewis and Peter Mitchell, eds., *Children's Early Understanding of Mind: Origins and Development* (Hillsdale, N.J.: Erlbaum, 1994), 47–70.

————, and Richard W. Byrne, eds., *Machiavellian Intelligence* (Oxford: Oxford University Press, 1988).

Wiener, Norbert, *Cybernetics; or, Control and Communication in the Animal and the Machine* (New York: Wiley, 1948).

Wittgenstein, Ludwig, *Philosophical Investigations* (Oxford: Blackwell, 1958).

Young, Andrew, "The Neuropsychology of Awareness," in Antii Revonsuo and Matti Kamppinen, *Consciousness in Philosophy and Cognitive Neuroscience* (Hillsdale, N.J.: Erlbaum, 1994), 173–203.